HOLY SMOKE

HOLY SMOKE

THE DAILY LIFE OF A RECTOR IN THE CITY OF LONDON

PETER MULLEN

British Library cataloguing in publication data
A catalogue record of this book is available from
The British Library

ISBN 0-9547157-0-5

To: The people of St Michael's and St Sepulchre's

Printed and bound in Great Britain by
Woolnough Bookbinding, Irthlingborough, Northants.

Contents

Lord Mayor's Chaplain   9

11th September: A Tale of Two Cities   15

Memorial Services in the City   19

Millennium Dome   22

The London Challenge   26

For Better or for Worse   30

Trying to Have a Holiday from the City Church   33

The Gospel of Political Correctness   37

The City Service   40

What is an Archbishop for?   47

The Golden Jubilee   51

Some Funerals are Funnier than Others   57

Livery or Liverish?   66

Can You Open a Bank Account in the City of London?   75

Over My Dead Body   78

New Age Yuppies Steal the Font   83

The Automatic Ecclesiastical Switchboard   87

Ghosts   93

Tatty Tate   96

Order of Service to Mark the Passing of the ASB   98

Let Us Now Praise Famous Men – and Women   104

The Rector: "A Conman Operating a Scam"   108

For the Fallen   111

In The Scrubs   117

Gaffes, Graces and Princes   120

What Have the Livery Companies Ever Done for Us?   126

Visiting Speakers   129

A Cup of Tea at the BBC   134

There Were Giants: A Recollection of Fr John Paul R.I.P.   137

Choirs and Places Where They Sing   140

"To Do a Good Action by Stealth and Have it
    Found Out by Accident"   147

Preface

In 1998, I was invited by the Bishop of London to become incumbent of two historic churches in the City of London. I knew this would be something of a culture shock, as my previous experience had been as a suburban curate in Leeds, a religious education teacher in Bolton and a country parson in Yorkshire on the site of the Battle of Marston Moor.

The job was what you might call a challenge. I was thrilled to have been given the opportunity, though the idea of the move from the broad acres to a house right opposite the Old Bailey and Bart's Hospital gave me a few sleepless nights. As a part-time journalist and writer, I had been in the habit of visiting London fairly regularly to see editors and publishers, and I had always hated the place: it seemed to me to be a vast and shapeless sprawl, dirty, noisy and uncouth. It was only when I actually came to live here that I felt the wonder of the City. The crucial difference was between having to travel to the capital and actually living here.

Immediately, I was pleasantly surprised. I found I adored being in the middle of this world-renowned civic and financial centre. My two churches are historic beauties, used by many livery companies, resounding with fine music and at the heart of the ceremonial and business life of the nation. It was wonderful to be able to walk to the National Gallery; to shop for meat at Smithfield Market, just around the corner; to have the choice of a dozen theatres and half a dozen concerts on free evenings –   of which there were soon increasingly few. I love the clubbability of the charitable livery companies and the powerful ancient rituals associated with the Lord Mayor, the Sheriffs, the Judges and the ancient traditions of governance in the great City. In a word, I quickly went native.

After a couple of years the Bishop came to St Michael's to preach and I told him with gleeful honesty: "This is not only the best job I've ever had. It's the best job I could ever imagine having."

In the pages that follow I have told a few tales out of my years as a City Rector. I hope they give the flavour of this amazing place and convey a little of the astonishing richness of the cultural life of the greatest City in the world.

PETER MULLEN
(Rector of St Michael's, Cornhill and St Sepulchre-without-Newgate and Chaplain to the Stock Exchange)

Lord Mayor's Chaplain

As soon as the letter arrived, I went shopping for a pair of shoes with silver buckles - and a three-cornered hat. The letter was from the Lord Mayor Elect asking me to be his Chaplain for his year of office. Academic and clerical outfitters' catalogues of exotic attire feature photographs of glamorous young clergymen, and these days clergywomen, wearing their banana-split smiles. On the opposite page there are pictures of dons trying to look thoughtful in what might seem indictable postures. By the time I'd paid for the fancy shoes, there was nothing left in the kitty for the hat. Luckily, almost accidentally, I picked one up for one pound-fifty in a joke shop in Salisbury and practised wearing it about that historic city. I hoped I might look like the Holy Fool, but by the way people stared I could tell they thought I was only a plain and simple fool.

Large brown envelopes began to arrive daily from Mansion House. These set out the various protocols to be followed by the Chaplain as he attended on the Lord Mayor. Some engagements were merely formal and required the usual evening dress. Others, such as the Lord Mayor's Banquet at The Guildhall, were described as state and these commanded the Chaplain to wear such an array of clothes that the aptest comment would be to say even Solomon in all his glory was not arrayed like me. Not just a black cassock, but over it a scarf and a Geneva gown. White gloves, preaching bands, the hat of course and Papageno's twinkly shoes.

The ancient City of London is divided into wards whose political representatives in the governing Corporation are common councilmen and aldermen. The councilmen are, as it were, the City's House of Commons and the aldermen the Lords. The Lord Mayor – whose office dates from the time of Henry Fitz Aylwin in AD 1192 – is elected each year from the Court of Aldermen. "Elected" is euphemism for a process that resembles an elegant form of buggin's turn. Everybody knows at least three years in advance who the next Lord Mayor is to be, but an election ceremony is held nonetheless in the Guildhall. Representatives from the more than a hundred Livery Companies fill the hall and listen to orations from the Town Crier and the senior judge at the Old Bailey – known as the Recorder – and other bewigged and gowned officials with romantic titles such as the Remembrancer, which sounds like a character from Brave New World. The name of the person who is to be Lord Mayor several years hence is called out first and the liverymen's chorus answers back, "Not yet". Then the name of the next year's Lord Mayor and the response is, "Later". At last the Lord Mayor is acclaimed by a unanimous, "Aye".

There is a piece of pure theatre called the Silent Ceremony, when the Guildhall is packed with aldermen, liverymen and common councilmen to watch in utter quiet while the incoming Lord Mayor subscribes to the Declaration of Loyalty. There is much exchanging of hats between him and the outgoing Mayor – disconcertingly referred to as the Late Lord Mayor. A solemn pantomime and the silence so intense it seems to hiss.

In thick November darkness in the very early hours of Friday morning I put on my state costume and walked the half mile from my Rectory to the Guildhall for the rehearsal for Lord Mayor's Day. The wet cobbles like a rocky shore at low tide. By the tall tower of Christchurch Greyfriars a single tree illuminated by the street lamp was the only dash of colour in the clinging blackness. City ceremonials always start with a drink, continue with several more and end with another – so that some guests have been known to be not merely in state but in a state. But at this early hour there was a rare concession to abstemiousness and the drink was coffee. Parked outside the Guildhall, like a scene from Cinderella, stood the 17th century State Coach and we practised getting into it. The only people who get to ride in the coach are the Sword-bearer, in his fur hat, the Mace-bearer, the Chaplain and the Lord Mayor himself. The ceremonial Sword and Mace are taken in there as well, so it is a rather cramped elegance. The procession of State Coach, marching pikemen and the two Sheriffs in their coaches, led by the City Marshall on horseback, set off for Mansion House, provoking a mixture of curiosity and irritation from the early motorists.

Bumping and rolling through the ancient streets of London town with their resounding names – Gresham Street, Cheapside and Poultry – awe is what one feels: awe and cramp. The Sword-bearer leant forward and whispered, "Tomorrow you'll have carrots for the horses under your seat. It's traditional". Once outside Mansion House, the Lord Mayor's official residence, we stopped and practised getting out of the coaches and on to the balcony from where, next day, we would watch the decorated floats and costumed marchers. A triangle of weighty history: the Bank of England, that "Old Lady of Threadneedle Street", the Royal Exchange, the Stock Exchange and Lloyds Bank, Cornhill where T.S. Eliot worked in the foreign exchange department:

O City, City...down King William Street to where St Mary Woolnoth kept the hours, with a dead sound on the final stroke of nine...St Magnus Martyr, inexplicable splendour of Ionian white and gold...Sweet Thames run softly till I end my song...

By this time the traffic had increased around our civic parade and car drivers were giving us un-civic black looks.

On Lord Mayor's Day we sat under the striped canopy on the balcony while less privileged mortals stood beneath in the wind and rain to watch the pageant: the regiments and their military bands, Life on the ocean wave...Men of Harlech...pride and nostalgia. Then the steel bands from Hackney and Brixton and the whirling dancers colourfully under-dressed for the weather. The fire brigade and the Red Cross. Police. Pensioners. Postmen. The single Lancaster bomber roaring the RAF's flypast.

I led the procession tremulously down the external staircase and got into the coach for the ride to the Law Courts. The Mace-bearer said, "It's OK – we've got the carrots". It teemed down all the way, but thousands of people from all over London and beyond stood on the pavements, cheered and waved flags. It wasn't a case of oiks doffing their caps at the toffs. Those cheering, rain-soaked people were celebrating something that gave them their own sense of identity. Despite the great egalitarian brainwashing that has gone on since the end of the Second World War and which has reached insane proportions recently, people still have an urge to defer to something or someone they esteem and value. And the quality of what you value shows you what you're worth. People will revere something: better a thousand-year-old mayoralty than a grade three celebrity.

The Law Courts are pure Gilbert and Sullivan and on this historic but light-hearted occasion the exalted legal principals grinned like characters from a Savoy opera. The new Lord Mayor was presented to the Lord Chief Justice and to the Recorder, whose speeches were erudite banter featuring the livelier remarks of the ancient Greek and Roman orators. Things were running late and I had ten seconds before the coach left for the return journey to grab from the ubiquitous attendants two glasses of Champagne to refresh my Lord Mayor before he must be out in the street again acknowledging his public. In fact, things were running very late and the Sword-bearer said that if we didn't get back to the reception soon, he would eat the ceremonial carrots provided for the horses.

On the Monday following the presentation there is always the Lord Mayor's Banquet at the Guildhall. The Chaplain is made to stand behind the throne, in state, while the hundreds of guests are received, among them the Prime Minister and the Archbishop of Canterbury. There are many other such banquets in the Mayoral calendar and I remember the best wine was served at the dinner for all the bishops and archbishops: Mansion House filled with a purple blur, clichéd ecclesiastical chit-chat and lashings of St Aubin Premiere Cru Bourgogne washed down with gallons of Chateau Malartic-Lagraviere Pessac-Leogman 1993.

Quite a contrast to the dinner which the Lord Mayor provides for the mayors of all the other London boroughs. Respectable toy-town civics for the most part, with just a dash of class warfare. Many of the mayors are from south of the river and some regard the City of London as the Great Satan that will be done away when the revolution comes. When these types are presented, they approach the Chair with smiles like acid indigestion and make their deep bows with cynical obsequiousness and sideways grins at their fellow-travelling comrades. Towards the end of that dinner, I passed some of this party as they staggered on the stairs. Some were on their way down, but a few were making their way back into the main hall. Conversation as follows:

"Aren't you going home?"

"Not yet. We're sticking around for a drop more of this f****** capitalist booze!"

You see quite a bit of the lumpen intelligentsia as the year goes on

12

– particularly among the clergy. A woman priest, all ironical and post-modern with clanking earrings and a sanctimoniousness of which Caiaphas would have been proud, bumped into me at the Lord Mayor's Breakfast, deep in the crypt in Guildhall, and when I asked her if she was enjoying herself said, "Oh it's all too white and middle class and male!" I wanted to christen her Esmeralda Salmonella.

But she drank the Lord Mayor's mulled wine and swallowed a plate-ful of his scrambled eggs and sausages even as she sneered. Another clergyman with a resplendent complexion and a handshake cold as the living dead told me with ferocious earnestness, "I regard myself as a prophet to the City. The City is the enemy, you know". This from a man who is out to a glittering livery dinner twice a week and whose church receives generous support from City institutions. Their hubris is terrifying. Their self-righteousness sickening. Beware the Scribes. If they don't like the City, why do they come to work here? Presumably to convert us according to their more excellent way.

I don't know what it is about this sort of clergyman. They don't see the deeply paradoxical nature of their position. Here they all are, priv-ileged members of an elite establishment, yet they talk as if they're liv-ing on a diet of locusts and wild honey. Worse, they completely lack insight into their own political prejudices. All these social-gospellers, class warriors – like personal composites of Uriah Heep and Mr Collins. The more senior the clergyman, the sharper the ideological reflex. An Archbishop came to address the Annual City Service at St Michael's and preached to the three hundred or so leading City businessmen there assembled: "Money is important, but it's not all-important."

As if Noddy should give lessons in story-telling to Enid Blyton! Did he think it was wisdom he was offering them? A Past Master of the Drapers' Company said to me privately afterwards, "'Money is not all-important'! Did he think we didn't know that? I tell you, in my Company we spend about two per cent of our income on wining and dining and the rest of our time in committee meetings trying to decide how to give the other ninety-eight per cent of it away."

And the Lord Mayor himself – it's not as if he spends his year float-ing from one banquet to the next in his limo with the number plate LMO. Sleeves actually get rolled up. How about his five o'clock in the

13

morning visit to Billingsgate fish market to meet the porters? Or the first Saturday in the New Year when he throws a fancy dress party for hundreds of children in Mansion House? One Lord Mayor, a few years back, displayed a rare gift for showing the Church Militant Tendency a thing or two. There is a tradition for the City Synod to present the Lord Mayor with a bible. This one graciously accepted their offer, but insisted the version he received should be that by William Tyndale. Tyndale's Bible was of course the prototype for the King James 1611 version, detested and abandoned by the modern clergy. Not only did that Lord Mayor ask for the traditional bible, but his speech of thanks was a lively seven-minute talk about Tyndale and his work as a translator. The modern clergymen sat with expressions that suggested acid indigestion.

People are constantly surprised to learn that the King James, or Authorised Version, is never used at St Paul's itself. They use some godforsaken modern version even for the big civic services. It's not quite true to say that the King James version is never used. One of the canons at St Paul's told me, "We only use it when the royalty come – awkward people like that". It is the perfect measure of the modern Church's contempt for its own tradition.

These senior clergymen, bishops and archbishops and the like, they speak from a great height but not, unfortunately, from any great depth. They are past masters of the missed opportunity. For example, when he was still Archbishop of Wales, the present Archbishop of Canterbury came to St Paul's Cathedral to preach to a nave packed with the great and the good. Here was a chance, literally, to influence them for God's sake. What we got from him instead was a twenty-minute exercise in theological obfuscation. As I walked down the steps, a chairman of one of the big banks smiled at me and said, "He doesn't always seem to distinguish between profundity and obscurantism, does he?"

We strolled off to Cutlers' Hall, where the company was more humane and the Chablis just right with the sea bass.

11th September:

A Tale of Two Cities

The day before the attack on the World Trade Center, I went to a conference at St Catherine's College, Oxford to which the Bishop of London had called the Diocesan clergy. It was the usual thing: a trendy yet clichéd title: Urban Ministry in a Time of Change. But what time is not a time of change for the trendy hierarchy of the Church of England? The times they are a changin' and they always were, always will be. That's what "time" means. Oxford. Dreaming spires over the legendary home of lost causes. Why does it prove so attractive to the more or less unreconstructed Stalinists who lectured us on our duty to the poor and the alienated – and the only remedies they offered were the failed unholy trinity of taxation, taxation, taxation; regulation, regulation, regulation; intervention, intervention, intervention? I looked down from the back of the lecture theatre and beheld in these churchy academics a virulent hatred for all our traditions and institutions and a petulant desire to remodel the world – and particularly our part of the Diocese of London – in the form of the Comintern.

The language employed by the Distinguished Speakers was straight out of the Marxian sociology of the 1960s: "developing structures"; "establishing hegemony"; "alienation of the proletariat"; "criteria of primacy", and so on.

But one has learnt to expect nothing better from ecclesiastical politicians. The worst of it was the church services. Three each day. Picture the scene: the beautiful medieval church of Holy Cross, just behind Merton's playing fields. How would you have ordered these services? Some fine organ music. Ancient and familiar prayers. Sermons that betrayed some whiff of intelligence. Come off it! We're talking about the contemporary Church of England. Not one service from the Prayer Book in three whole days. Let me deal with the music first and get it out of the way. Over in the Lady Chapel an out-of-tune piano which was itself out of tune with an accidental oboe; a violin that sounded like a cat crying because someone had spilt hot milk on its private parts; and a sempiternal, grinning modern clergyman – I knew he was a clergyman because he was wielding a guitar.

We sang banal and meaningless choruses to plinky plonky music of the Jesus goes to toy-town variety. Then we sat through horrific sermons. I'm not making this up. The Bishop of Stepney told us that doctrine doesn't matter: "All you need is love" - reminding us of The Beatles. Gosh! There is nothing more out of date, is there, than an out of date trendy? Now I don't want to frighten readers unnecessarily, but I must tell you what the Bishop said next. He said, "In a few minutes, we shall offer one another a sign of peace. I don't want to see handshakes. I want to see you hugging one another. And then I'll tell you something else I want you to do." Those of a nervous disposition, please feel free to close this book now.

Well, the so-called "Peace" was announced, and all hell broke loose. Five full minutes of people wandering about sacred space proffering more or less sentimental or lewd greetings. When I was set upon by a vast and enthusiastic lady, I did my usual escape act, fell to my knees and, when she tried to lift me bodily into the furnace of her embrace, exclaimed, "No, thank you, madam, I'm English." Now with trepidation I come to the "something else" which the Bishop of Stepney had promised to ask us to do. Well, it makes you think... I had been dreading this for six or seven minutes, as one in the dentist's waiting room. He bawled out: "I want you to turn to the person next to you and put your hands on his or her shoulders..." - his or her – funny isn't it how political correctness survives all atrocities? – and say three times, "You are everlastingly loved."

Luckily, I found myself not next to Deaconess Blenkinsop with the hot lips and fiery breath, but Father Alan Griffin who is Rector of St James, Garlickhythe – the national headquarters of the Prayer Book Society. I clenched my teeth and whispered, "You are everlastingly loved." Alan placed his hands affectionately on my shoulders and said, so far as I could interpret, "It's all right, Peter. I'll buy you a pint later." This was by no means the end of the embarrassment. The Bishop of Stepney went into full pantomime mode. "That's not enough. Again! Louder!" And he cocked his hand behind his ear, as Bruce Forsyth used to do on The Generation Game: "Nice to see you. To see you, nice!" I feared this was going to develop: "Where's the Archdeacon? Has any

16

little boy or little girl seen the Archdeacon?" Followed by a great chorus of "He's BEHIND you!" All this folly could, I suppose, be forgiv-
en – except that the date was 11th September. After that ludicrous service – really a disservice – I had a light lunch and walked into Oxford.
I went into Blackwells and bought some books then returned to my
room and read for the rest of the afternoon. At six o'clock I went, duty
bound, back to church again for more of the horrific Noddy liturgy.
Only this time the priest – with his shaved head, his designer stubble,
leather jacket and lisp - was telling us about the attacks on the USA.
Then guess what? Silence perhaps? Tears? The General Confession?
Not at all. But straight into more of the plinky plonky, happy clappy
music and Jesus goes to toy-town again.

The trouble is that this diminished sort of spirituality, this bankrupt,
dumbed down, blasphemous style of worship could not do justice to
the terrible events that were unfolding. There were, however, two
redeeming features. The Bishop of London gave a pertinent, off the
cuff, short address which was a masterpiece in précis. Then Father
Chad Varah, ninety this year, founder of The Samaritans, burst forth
with, "In the midst of life we are in death. Of whom may we seek for
succour, but of thee O Lord, who for our sins art justly displeased..."
It cut through the whole out of tune, plinky plonky, earringed, sentimental, hug one another, you are everlastingly bored charade like a hot
sabre through the flesh of roast piglet.

I escaped from that conference and came back on the first train to
London. I put on a Requiem Mass at twenty-four hours' notice, and
250 people turned up for it. City types can be a bit raucous, insensitive,
philistine. I swear no one moved a muscle for the thirty-five minutes
from start to finish. No mobile phone went off. There was an atmosphere of the most intense reverence. Here were people, largely un-
churched, with more of an idea of the holy than the cream of London's
clergy at a religious conference.

And we had no jogging for Jesus music; no smarmy grins; no creepy
introduction of the "We are living in tragic times" variety. No super-
fluous ecclesiastical chat of any kind. I started off with Requiem aeter-
nam dona eis, Domine, et lux perpetuam luceat eis...I know that my
Redeemer liveth, and that he shall stand upon the earth at the latter
day; and though after my skin worms destroy this body, yet in my flesh

17

shall I see God... The sun burst suddenly through the stained glass and illuminated the altar spectrally. When it was over, I stood at the door as the City workers walked out, many sobbing silently, and went back to their desks.

Opposite my Rectory stands the new headquarters of Merrill Lynch, the huge merchant bank. Its main trading floor is the biggest in Europe – about a hundred yards long. Three of Merrill's employees were killed in the attack on the Twin Towers and their chief executive asked for a Memorial Service for them to be held in St Sepulchre's.

For this, three tall candles dominated the transept and the church was again filled with City workers. There were prayers and readings, a couple of well-known hymns. A leading soprano from our choir began the first verse of The Star Spangled Banner. Then all those who could quell the lump in their throat sufficiently joined in. It was an atmosphere of deep reverence and intense resolve.

The Requiem Mass and that Memorial Service just go to show that even in the 21st century you can still be authentically religious – provided you start by ignoring most of the Church of England.

Memorial Services in the City

There are very few funerals in the City of London. This is because we have no resident population. Once everyone has gone home on Friday evening, the place is as serene as a remote village. The pubs and restaurants close for the weekend and the peace and quiet are palpable. But these Memorial Services are not what they used to be. Not many years ago, the church would be packed with dignified men in pinstripes and elegant ladies in hats and veils, come to pay last respects to such as Sir Robert, Chairman of Bigbank Ltd. They would sing with lusty restraint hymns such as Jerusalem and The Day Thou Gavest Lord Is Ended. The reading would be from the Bible, of course: something familiar and comfortingly apt, such as "And God shall wipe away all tears from their eyes". It was rare to have a secular reading, but if there was to be one it would be after the style of John Donne's matchless sonnet Death Be Not Proud. The Rector would give a short address. We would listen as the choir sang Nunc Dimittis and then everyone would repair to a local livery hall for drinks and canapes.

Occasionally, I get asked for a Memorial Service old style, but increasingly something - I am struggling for words - more pop and pagan is required. Dress multifarious informal. Organ music before the service might include "Some of Bob's favourite ballads": anything from Singing In The Rain, or The Beatles' maudlin Yesterday; and now and then they will import the bank's audio system and belt out something off the top of the Richter Scale by Sid Filth that makes you think of a pile-driver screwing a score of metal dustbins.

New style Memorial Services are above all talkative. Three or even four of the deceased's family and friends will get up to "offer a tribute". I know we must all respect De mortuis nil nisi bonum, but these tributes would fall foul of the Trades Descriptions Act. We are asked to recall that Bob, "or 'Chuckles' as he liked to be called on account of his infectious giggle", was a married archangel with four children and fifteen grandchildren. He was brilliant in his work at the bank where everybody loved him. Like hell he was! Many in church wince as they remember how he used to growl at the juniors and make them cry. And if he was really so brilliant, why was he made redundant?

At home he had the bonhomie of Alistair Sim playing the reformed Scrooge. He kept a superb table, never failed to bring his wife flowers every Friday and was always effervescently happy. Well, Aristotle said, "Call not a man happy until he's dead", but I hardly thought the great philosopher meant that a man had to wait until after he'd died to effect such a remarkable character change - from curmudgeon to comedian, from reclusive skinflint to "life and soul of any party". As for constantly taking the children sailing, they, grown up now and sitting on the front row, recall cringingly that the only time he took them on a boat was to threaten to chuck them over the side if they didn't stop whining. I suppose it's a blessing that most of the speakers haven't the faintest notion how to project the voice and so the sentimental drivel cannot be heard at all beyond the third row.

But these schmaltzy eulogies are not the worst part of the service - not by any means. There is among modern, wholly un-churched mourners still the desire to "do something religious". Not The Lord's My Shepherd or How Lovely Is Thy Dwelling Place, O Lord Of Hosts. These mainstays of English religion are nowadays quite unknown. What is not unknown is some sentimental, vaguely middle-eastern, doggerel by someone with a name like Alhacca Armanaleg: "O look up to where the white night owl stares and think that this also will pass. There's an ocean of grass so sit on your..."

Such sickly drivel that it might have been produced for a chocolate box by the combined efforts of Barbara Cartland and Patience Strong. I love it if, in the middle of this guff, a couple of mobile phones go off - especially when the tune they are bleeping happens to be Jesu, Joy Of Man's Desiring or the Toccata & Fugue in D Minor by Bach: ironically, the only bit of real religion in the whole hideous show provided by a post-modern icon of consumerism! The difference between the old services and the new, is quite simply that, in the former, as befits a church service, the centre of reference was God; in the latter, the centre of attention is the narcissistic, moonshine emotionality of the mob as it were at a Diana-Fest. Memorial Services have become consumer affairs, part of the whole mindless, chuck-away me-ism of the contemporary junk culture.

There are moments so crass as to be unbeatable. A distant cousin might slouch to the lectern and remind us that, "As well as being

Master of the Guild of Confectioners, Bob was, in his younger days, something of a ladies' man." Cue for a woman in a flowery dress hinting at circumnavigation to step forward and warble, If I Knew You Were Coming, I'd Have Baked A Cake.

Since we're into consumerism, I'd like to offer a full portfolio of Memorial Services, including an idea of my own. Here comes his elder brother: "I've known Bob all my life, of course..." [this works best if you can hear it in the voice of Alan Bennett] "... he worked day and night to support his family. Straight home from the bank, and, after saying, 'Thanks for a nice bit of tea, mother', he'd slip into his burglar togs and break into the LIFFE building.

"And, when he got too frail for organised crime and insider-trading, he'd still cheerfully contrive to fiddle his expenses every week. But this was when Bob came to rely on his many hobbies. As well as being a keen canasta player, he was, as some of his dearest friends know, a lifelong paedophile. After his retirement, and before his final illness rendered him too frail to operate the video remote-control, I'd go round to his house of an evening and, while we sipped dry martinis, Bob would show me his wonderful collection of literally thousands of photographs of little boys and girls in indecent poses."

But no, things have got so ridiculous that satire is impossible. Already, we've fallen a lot further than you think towards the everlasting bonfire.

Millennium Dome

A senior banker in the City met me in the Jamaica Inn just before Christmas 1999 and said, "I reckon they've really cocked up the arrangements for the new millennium. We'll just have to try to get it right next time!" The City shut down on Christmas Eve anyhow, as it always does. So there were no natives, as it were, in town to celebrate Millennium Eve. I sat in the Rectory all that afternoon, listening to the tramp of footsteps outside as thousands made their sentimental way down via Ludgate Hill and Blackfriars to try to secure a position on the Embankment from which to watch the firework display. By ten o'clock in the evening, you couldn't get anywhere near. All the pubs were shut because, so a barmaid told me, staff were demanding five times the usual rate to turn out on such an auspicious night.

It was not what you would call festive. Faces in the crowd were rather lugubrious. The banker was right. It was pretty much a shambles. Drab. I returned home, opened a bottle, and sat down to watch the doings at the Dome on television. At the witching hour we were presented with the unforgettable vulgarity and crass insubordination of Tony and Cherie Blair making the Queen join hands with them in the Dome and sing Auld Lang Syne. The Bishop of London had already given me his opinion about the Millennium Dome, its dumbed down contents – the so-called Body Zone in particular. "Now," said the Rt Rev'd and Rt Hon Richard Chartres, "the people of England have the opportunity to queue to crawl up a gigantic version of their own primary orifice and disappear."

I thought the best thing to do would be to offer the City a Millennium Sermon, or sort of anti-sermon, extolling the banality of that ludicrous monument at Greenwich:

And it came to pass in those days that there arose in the land of Lud, in the days of the Great Tone, a son of man which was called Man-Del-Son, a left-handed man and musical; and the number of the man was 666. And behold, Man-Del-Son toiled mightily and verily he did spin. He that hath ears to hear, let him hear. And Man-Del-Son dwelt in the palace of the Great Tone, and lo it came to pass that he went in unto the King and saith, "O Tone, live forever, thou and thy wife and thy children and thy children which are yet to be."

And the Great Tone answering spake unto him and said, "Thou art my good and faithful servant, what wouldst thou that I should have done?"

And Man-Del-Son, entreating him, spake softly unto him and saith, "Thou O Tone art mighty in the land, and thy name goeth forth among all the people which praise thee for thy dab-handedness with the smoke and mirrors. And lo, thy people which do unto thee true and faithful homage, would make unto thee an image of costly stuff and set it up that all men might know of thy glory and thy wisdom which exceedeth that of all men that have been in the days of our forefathers."

When the Great Tone heard this he was glad and his heart leapt within his breast, and he saith unto him that was called Man-del-Son, "Thou hast well-spoken. It is meet and right that men should honour my name above that of all our forefathers. Speak and let it be known what manner of image thou wouldst set up, that all peoples, nations and languages might come and pay me homage."

And Man-Del-Son spake unto the Great Tone and said, "Lo, I would make unto thee a golden calf, Sire."

But the Tone was wroth and he would fain smite his servant in the hind parts; and he saith, "Verily, look, c'mon Peter, aha! Like, well, some other guy did this golden calf bit way back."

And Man-Del-Son cast in his mind what manner of salutation this might be, and when he saw that his master was exceeding wroth, he was sore afraid. But in him was guile, and he was a man crafty above all craftiness. And he fell down on his face and spake unto the Tone, "Verily I will make unto thee a great Dome."

And the Tone was astonished and repented him of the evil and saith, "Go and do even as thou hast spoken."

And he went out from thence and gathered together all the soothsayers and the magicians and the physicians of that which is called "spin"; and behold they assembled a great company of labourers and did charge them to tarry not but haste and make ready this thing which should come to pass. And in the latter days, behold the Dome was raised up by the riverside and great was the press of the people to see what manner of thing it should be; for they said, "What is this thing that is called 'Dome'? Lo, we cannot tell what it is." But when the

Great Tone saw it he was glad and rejoiced with exceeding great joy. And he gathered together his chariots and his horsemen and a great company of physicians of that which is called "spin" and they did cause the name of the Dome to be noised throughout the land. And the Tone called a solemn feast day at the beginning of the year and caused them to blow up the trumpets in the new moon. And at the appointed hour he did go into the Dome, he and his manservants and his maidservants and his whole household; and he went even into the midst of it and said, "Behold thy Great Tone and the Dome which is built in my name. See ye that there is none like unto me, no not in all your forefathers which were once and have now fallen asleep!" And they all with one accord began to make merry.

And it came to pass that when the prophet of the Lord heard the uproar of the people, he did gird up his loins and enter into the Dome, even into the midst of it where stood the Great Tone. And he did raise his staff and cry aloud, "What is this that thou hast done? What is this thing that thou callest 'Dome'? Behold it is an idol and an offence before the Lord God! And thou, O Tone, because thou hast done this thing and caused this abomination of desolation to be set up, thou shalt be brought low; thou and thy whole household and thy physicians which deal in 'spin'. And the Lord will altogether remove thy name from the land, because thou hast forgotten the name of the Lord and hearkeneth not to his commandment, 'Thou shalt have no other gods before me'."

And lo, the Tone was much discomfited and his face turneth white as the snow. And he would feign have lain hands on the prophet of the Lord and made away with him; but he was afraid for the tumult of the people.

And the prophet of the Lord cried in a loud voice and he brake the baubles and trinkets which Man-Del-Son had set up; and he struck mightily with his staff the great idol which was called "Body Zone" wherein were wont to crawl both men and women, into the members and passages thereof, even into the back parts. And behold it fell, and great was the fall of it. And he did curse the music which is called "abominable" and the lights which flash and he said, "Because thou hast done this thing thou art curst above all thy forefathers. This thing that thou callest 'Dome' it is but a vain thing and an idol of thine own invention wherein thou seest thine own glory and not the glory of the Lord.

"Thou rememberest not this solemn feast day and what it doth signify. Behold, it is the feast day of the Lord and this New Year is an homage to his name, even unto two thousand years from the day wherein He was born. This that thou callest 'Dome' is an abomination before the Lord and thou dost blaspheme his holy name. There is one Dome in the City and it is that which men call 'St Paul's'. It is no thing newfangled, but it abideth these three hundred one score and ten years; and even now it proclaimeth the New Year of our Lord and our God. Get thee thence therefore and repent ye of your sins, put on sackcloth and ashes and call ye upon the name of the Lord. And it may be that he will return and give you his blessing."

And all the people said, "Amen."

The London Challenge

The Church of England authorities are addicted to change. So perpetual change is foisted on the parishes. They seem to forget – or do they? – that perpetual revolution was the chief means by which Leninists and Trotskyists aimed to destabilise the social order. And this depressing tactic works: if you keep moving the goal-posts and redrawing the boundary lines, it becomes impossible to play a game of football. Over these last thirty years, we have seen the deliberate abandonment of the Authorised Version of the Bible and The Book of Common Prayer; the altars moved; the traditional hymns replaced by empty-headed choruses; worse, the traditional teaching about sin and redemption sidelined in favour of religion as psychotherapy, theology as mere wetness. It's a sort of emotional incontinence: you turn up at a Deanery or Diocesan Service and you find that the traditional prayers have been ditched in favour of Post-Diana, touchy-feely drippiness: ...that we may be in touch with our inner selves.

Now this pace of perpetual change has been deliberately accelerated and set to disco music. The Diocese of London has produced this pantomime called The London Challenge. Glossy booklets; embarrassing admonitions to the clergy; a meeting of all the parsons at the evangelical shrine or talkative Prot shop, All Souls, Langham Place for a pep talk, a video presentation, more rock music and gallons of moral blackmail. The conductor/chorus master stared at us all the time with a sort of lugubrious glee: imagine the expression on the face of Mr Sowerberry having just heard he had won the National Lottery. But I'm repeating ancient history. The London Challenge has now moved into phase two. Parishes are being asked to receive visitors from other parishes to observe and evaluate the extent to which congregations are – in the jargon – responding to the London Challenge. The impression is of visits by the nit nurse or perhaps the thought police.

There are varieties of futility and then there are the Church of England authorities. Let me give you the craziest example. Clergy get asked to go on a great number of meaningless conferences and courses; all of them a waste of time; all of them merely aping the secular obsession with management techniques. But once I was astounded when I received an invitation from the diocese to go on a conference called Work/Life Balance: Learning to say NO with confidence and compassion. Unbelievably, the explicit purpose of this conference was to teach busy parsons how to refuse to go on conferences. I simply wrote back and said, I know how to say NO already, thanks.

Well, what sorts of things are being officially recommended as adequate responses to The London Challenge. Let me offer those of you with a high cringe threshold a few examples from the official (shall I say?) literature. "On London Challenge Day – Oh yes, there's going to be one! – have your group decorate plain biscuits with icing, sprinkles and small sweets to share with the congregation at coffee time". Coffee time? What's that? It goes on: "Enjoy being able to have fun together!"

Well, if you get sick of Playschool, there are alternatives. For instance: "Why not try dancing for the Lord? It is a way to enhance worship by interpreting worship songs with movement. Using a sign language can help interpret the words of a song. Make the signs bigger to be more of a dance movement". This is Game for a Laugh translated to the chancel. That last recommendation is followed by some information which tells us a lot about how the church authorities assess our intelligence. They say: "Signing can be useful if you have deaf members of your church." Pardon? Gerraway! Then they say: "Some children learn through visual means." Can this really be true? It says: "What about a worshipful line dance or a Christian conga or a jive-for Jesus?" I was relieved though to see the further advice: "The aim is not to shock people...be modest in what you wear so that people can focus on God and not be distracted by the dancers' attire."

Don't imagine the intellectual content of The London Challenge is absolute zero. We are encouraged to interview a parishioner as part of the service. They tell us how to do this: "There should be eye contact between you both. A clip board is permissible for the interviewer." Now the next instruction chillingly tells us a lot about the authoritarianism behind all this drivel: "If using a microphone, keep hold of it yourself. Even if your guest tries to take it, keep a firm grasp. This ensures that you have the control."

We are told not to value tried and trusted ways of doing things. It says: "Deepen relationships with one another, regardless of our own traditions." That is exactly how an iconoclastic secularist or a militant

27

atheist would choose to destroy the Church – by abolishing its traditions. The London Challenge also instructs us as to what our politics should be: "Pray that all people, whatever their race, creed, colour or gender may live in harmony with one another and be in the forefront of promoting social justice...consider world development issues...a fair distribution of wealth...Pray for those who work in race relations." This is of course only political correctness tacked on to the failed collectivist social agenda which our rulers in the General Synod have tried to thrust on us for a generation in countless official reports on everything from glue-sniffing to the hydrogen bomb.

The hard politics sits awkwardly alongside the general touchy-feeliness of the programme. But then psychopathy and sentimentality always go together. Listen to this: "Each member of the community will be bringing with them their story/history and culture..." Culture? What culture? Jiving for Jesus? The decoration of small biscuits with icing while, of course, making sure not to lose your grip on the microphone? It continues: "their culture and their family/work/situation/interests. If all these are valued and used, the image of Christ which emerges will have a depth of reality and vibrancy which will not be able to be ignored."

Apart from the atrocious grammar, what needs to be said about all that is that it has nothing to do with the Christian faith. In fact, it is its opposite. The image of Christ does not emerge out of an oil can of psychobabble. Christ is proclaimed in the real Bible and received in the Blessed Sacrament. The London Challenge's depiction of what human beings are is not merely demeaning, insulting and offensive; but, because we are taught that human beings are made in the image of God, it is frankly blasphemous and insane. Line dancing and cutting out little bits of blue paper and sticking them on larger bits of yellow paper has nothing to do with what should go on in church. The worship and apprehension of God has to be practised attentively, with dignity, with the best we can bring, with the beauty of holiness. You are here to kneel where prayer has been valid.

Of course, the bottom line in any guff put out by the authorities is usually a financial one. And so it is with The London Challenge. Behind all the mawkish talk, we are told bluntly that after next year the London churches will receive nothing from central funds towards the upkeep of the parsons. This is because the authorities have screwed up central investments for decades and sold off all the stylish vicarages for a song.

After thirty years spent destroying all our treasures and supplanting them with a never-ending series of mindless innovation, this, The London Challenge, is the final shambles to which they hope to reduce us. Reading the glossy brochure and the pages of instructions you might feel justified in exclaiming, So the gates of hell have prevailed, then?

For Better or for Worse

Springtime is the most popular time to get married. St Michael's is a magnificent Wren church in the heart of the City and well-placed among the livery halls for smart receptions, so we have quite a few weddings booked. I hope I don't have to endure a repeat of last year's shenanigans. A couple came in off the street and asked if they might be allowed to make "alternative vows". You wonder what's coming next: do they want to replace "Till death us do part" with "...until a week on Tuesday"? Not quite. He, with the David Beckham haircut and clothing hanging about him in like manner, wanted to stand at the chancel steps and begin his lifelong vows with the immortal words, "Ever since we met last year in the disco..." This is the sort of degraded demotic that ought to qualify the bloke for a place on the Liturgical Commission, inventing new services for the trendy vicars. We didn't get as far as her reply. They took kindly enough to my advice - "Sorry, dears, this is the Church of England. Have you tried Blind Date?" - and shoved off. For the lesson, the favourite always used to be the miraculous chapter from St Paul ending with, "....and the greatest of these is love". Or else something luscious and sensual from the Old Testament's Song of Songs:

"Thou hast ravished my heart. Thou hast ravished my heart with one of thine eyes, with one chain of thy neck. How fair is thy love! How much better is thy love than wine, and the smell of thine ointments than all spices!"

But recent trends bear out G.K. Chesterton's warning that, "When men stop believing in God, they don't believe in nothing – they believe in anything". Couples increasingly ask if they might read the bum-clenchingly awful Invitation by someone with the preposterous name of Oriah Mountain Dreamer. This starts by hoping that the bride has not been "shrivelled and closed". No doubt the bridegroom hopes not too! It goes on to wonder whether the couple have "touched the centre of their own sorrow". This is at a wedding, mind you, not a wake!

And then, "I want to know if you will stand in the centre of the fire with me". But won't her dress melt? And "I want to know what sustains you from the inside" - to which the only possible response is

"Tripe and onions, love". But the best line must be, "I want to know if you can get up, after the night of grief and despair, weary and bruised to the bone". Good grief - it's going to be a rough honeymoon!

We use the old book at St Michael's, so we don't go in for any of that crooning sentimental guff you find in the new Common Worship - hideously mawkish phrases such as, "All that I am I give to you". What, does he give her his indigestion and bad temper? Then, incredibly, the priest prays: "Let them be tender with each other's dreams." It sounds like a schmaltzy song title by Andrew Lloyd Webber. I think there should be a rubric printed at this point in bold type in the margin of that godforsaken new worship book: "The congregation shall here throw up – bride's family's side first." The numbskull liturgical revisers never tire of telling the clergy that we have to modernise because the old Prayer Book wedding service is not relevant to our generation. That's patronising rubbish. How dare they tell today's young couples that this lovely, heartfelt traditional language is beyond them? It's not even true. In the last three years, we have held eighteen weddings, all from the 1662 book, and every couple has stayed to become regular members of the congregation.

But there's no limit to the banality and paucity of imagination of those who devise new marriage services. I mean, consider this. For hundreds of years the bridegroom said, "With this ring I thee wed". Those words go back to the time of Chaucer when they were spoken at the church door. I have heard them at weddings for thirty years and I can't think of a more moving utterance: six words of one syllable which exactly fit the movement of the placing of the ring on the bride's finger. This is lucid, spiritual poetry of great beauty. So what have the revisers done? Replaced those six enchanted words with eleven in the tedious, tin-eared phrase, "I give you this ring as a sign of our marriage". The revision is an act of cultural vandalism and sacrilege. Besides, it's a piece of sheer nonsense. I mean, you don't have to be Wittgenstein to see that, if he has to tell her that the ring is a sign, it means the sign isn't working.

The marvellous thing about the old Solemnisation of Matrimony is that it gives the lie to the accusation that the Christian faith is puritanical and anti-sex. In an ecstatic phrase, the bridegroom says to his bride, "With my body I thee worship." And, whereas the supposedly

relevant modern version is just one long catalogue of sentimental effu-
sions and disembodied evasions of sex, the old book is not afraid to
confront the reality: "carnal lusts and appetites…as a remedy against
sin and to avoid fornication", and all.

The clergy are human too. If anyone doubts the extreme pertinence
of carnal lusts and appetites, let him only think of the perspective of
the Parson as he stands on the chancel step and the voluptuous bride
kneels before him revealing a cleavage like King Solomon's Mines!

Somewhere among the corny jokes about letting them have any
hymns they like apart from Through the Night of Doubt and Sorrow
and Fight the Good Fight, there is the irresistible temptation to get the
giggles. I remember, for instance, standing in my place on the chancel
step and hearing - and watching - the biggest bridesmaid since the air-
craft-carrier Ark Royal boom out that line in Praise My Soul, "Well my
feeble frame He knows". Well, I'm sure He does.

What to say in the Address? That the wedding is a sacrament which
really does pour upon the couple the grace of God to help them till
death do them part. But it's also meant to be a cheerful occasion, so a
story or two helps. Here's one that always goes down well. The bridegroom went to see the vicar to arrange his wedding. The vicar asked
him, "Do you want the old service or the new one?"

The young man said he thought he would prefer the new one. On his
wedding day, he was driving to church through a thunderstorm and his
car got stuck in the flood. Nothing for it but to get out and push.
Unfortunately, this ensured that the trouser bottoms of his morning suit
were soaking wet. So he rolled them up. He arrived at church late and
the vicar was already standing in front of the bride on the chancel step.
When he saw the bridegroom coming up the aisle with his trousers
rolled up, he called out, "Pull your trousers down!"

To which the bridegroom replied, "You know, vicar, I think I'll have
the old service after all!"

I try to send them off with some sound advice: "Don't go too far on
the first night." At this the choir titters and the knicker elastic of the
maiden aunts snaps. You have to pause for just the right number of seconds and then add very solemnly, "My wife and I went as far as
Llandudno - and it was far too far…"

Trying to Have a Holiday from the City Church

Should a City Rector become a temporary atheist during the month of August? It's a serious question. I mean, for the rest of the year I look forward to going to our own church with exquisite pleasure. I tell people: "It's wonderful. It's as if you've died and gone to heaven!" Real words and real music, you see. None of the jogging for Jesus stuff they do in most churches these days. Well, we went to Hereford for our holidays and I thought that surely the ancient and venerable cathedral there might be a place where there was a traditional service and no nonsense. Alas! I offer you this reflection on my experience:

> Who are these with wings like frogs
> Who flap around in churchy togs,
> And offer us a rusty saw,
> As if we had not heard before
> That money will not save our soul?
> This preacher's dug himself a hole.
> He tells us we should turn to God,
> But never stops to think it odd
> We know we should be better men:
> The problem is of how and when.
> If we could be good by our will,
> Then Christ need ne'er have suffered ill.
> The Creed they use is hugely risible –
> Making unseen to mean invisible.
> Then when he comes to intercede
> It's quite enough to make us plead
> For silence rather than his manner
> Of making petition for Havana:
> Who lives in Hereford and prays for Fidel
> Has a perspective worse than Dingly Dell.

33

Prays for parishes in consternation
Of   "pastoral reorganisation".
What purpose in these weasel words?
Look, Father, tell it to the birds,
Or speak as we speak in the town –
You mean it's churches being closed down;
And that's not gospel, that's not funny,
But Church Commissioners wasting money.
The sermon over, and on our knees,
He offers us "a sign of peace",
And suddenly all hell breaks loose
With salutations, lewd, diffuse:
They grab your hand, they slap your back,
And squeeze so hard your ribs might crack;
These assailants don't even know your name,
But instant intimacy is their game.
So fall to the floor, cower, kneel
To dodge that smiley touchy feel.
Then music: ah mein Vater, Mutter –
This schtinking schtuff is by John Rutter!
No words of judgement will afford –
It's like "Come into the garden, Lord".
I'll tear my hymnbook, run and hide
Rather than do this palais glide.
Now at this Eucharistic Feast
We need the altar in the east;
But here they put it in the middle
(Surely a psychological fiddle?)
Declaring it's the proper thing
To have all standing in a ring,
Pretending this is "more inclusive" –
(Actually, it's most exclusive):
To make a circle, to put it crude,
Is by circumference to exclude
Not only the traditional bod,
But transcendence – bluntly, God.
Every cathedral, every church

Of which you care to make research,
Shows this very same disgrace –
The abolition of sacred space.
All over Europe this is done;
And wheresoever God is gone,
Now that there's no holy fear,
Satan is the victor here.
It's atheism, but by stealth –
Destruction to the soul's good health.
Where has true religion gone –
That mystery so near the bone?
The unutterable sense of the beyond
Turned into something fey and fond
By modern churchmen throughout the land,
Banal, bathetic, bloodless, bland,
Bureaucratic, sentimental,
Euphemistic, detrimental
To the sense we covet most –
That haunting by the Holy Ghost.
How dare they still use words like Lord
When all their thrust, their every word
Is utilitarian, un-pneumatic,
And God himself made democratic,
Preferring not an hierarch priest,
But a "president" at this dumbed-down feast.
He's reading from a PC Bible;
His every word a blatant libel
Of Christ, of God, our Prince, our King
Served by some vain, elected thing.
But let us ask, What is church for?
It's to be on earth an open door,
A ladder leading up to heaven;
Its rungs the sacraments, all seven.
Here we may hear the holy word,
But not from a version that's absurd.
Nor give us doctrine that's all wrong,

And sermons out of Patience Strong
By parsonical, Pelagian chaps
Who would pull us up by our bootstraps.
No we come to Mass this day
To learn our sins are done away.
That is the gospel of good news
To all who kneel in stalls or pews.
The beauty of holiness must abound
In silence, in ecstatic sound;
We should be like that Moses bod
When he looked on the face of God.
There should be joy; there must be fear
As we attend the Godhead here
Who gives to us who have no merit
Blessings by the Holy Spirit.
We leave as new, regenerate men:
Lift up your hearts and shout, Amen.

The Gospel of Political Correctness

The way the bishops and the General Synod slavishly follow secular fashions and fads – only like some prince consort, one dutiful step behind – we shall soon be called upon to abandon all those rich biblical tales and preach the gospel of political correctness. What might this trendy gospel contain?

If the gospels had not been written when they were, they could certainly not be written today – not with all their talk about cripples, deaf and dumb and blind people.

Imagine: a recently discovered fragment of a politically correct gospel. What it would have to say to fit the social fashions and trends of our times might be something like this...

And it came to pass that a certain lawyer enquired of him and said, "What must a man do to be politically correct, and what are the means thereof?"

And he saith, "Thou hast the commandments: thou shalt not be racist; neither shalt thou be sexist; thou shalt not smoke; thou shalt not wear a coat of fur nor hunt with hounds; and if a man ask ought of thee, thou shalt observe equal opportunities. Ye have heard it said, Take no thought for what ye shall eat or what she shall drink or wherewithal ye shall be clothed, but I say unto thee, take thought for what thou eatest and what thou drinkest: thou shalt keep the low fat diet and see that thou drinkest no more than the whiff of the serving maid's apron. Thou shalt consume five pieces of fruit every day of thy life, that thy days may be long in the land which the Lord thy God giveth thee. Consider not the lilies of the field and how they grow, but take thought for the designer clobber that thou dost put on. Remember not the Sabbath day to keep it holy: six days shalt thou labour and do all thy work, and on the seventh thou shalt go shopping."

And seeing the multitudes, he went up into a mountain, and he opened his mouth and taught them, saying, "Blessed are they that mourn, for they shall be compensated. Blessed are they that suffer from post-traumatic stress disorder, for they shall be counselled. Blessed are the illegal immigrants, for they shall inherit the earth. Blessed are the environmentalists, for they shall have their propaganda taught for free in the schools as if it were holy gospel. Blessed are ye when men shall say all manner of vain things against you, for then ye shall sue them. Blessed are the lawyers, for lo their pockets shall be filled. Blessed are the underprivileged, for they shall receive benefits. Blessed are the impure in heart, for there is a lot of entertainment for them on video and late-night telly."

As they drew near Sidon and the region about Tyre, there cometh a man visually-challenged, even as visually-challenged as a bat, beseeching him. And he spake unto them in his doctrine, saying, "Can the partially-sighted lead the partially-sighted?" And behold they bring unto him one which was hearing-impaired, saying, "This man is exceeding hearing-impaired, even as hearing-impaired as a post." And he saith, "Get thee a loop system as the equal access regulations command thee." And they came to Jericho and the multitudes pressed upon him. And behold Zacchaeus, an over-privileged man which also was vertically-challenged, climbed up into a sycamore tree to see him. And he besought him to come down and when he hath done so he gave the half of his goods to the disadvantaged and socially-excluded people from the inner city.

And the third day there was a wedding at Cana in Galilee, and his mother was there. And when they wanted unfermented grape juice, his mother saith, "They have no unfermented grape juice." And there were set there six water pots containing twenty or thirty litres apiece. And he saith, "Draw out now and bear unto caterer." And they bore it. When the caterer had tasted the water that was made unfermented grape juice and knew not whence it was, but the holiday-relief employees which drew the water knew, he saith, "Every man at the beginning doth set forth good unfermented grape juice and when men have well-drunk, then that which is worse: but thou hast kept the good unfermented grape juice until now."

And they bring unto him one who hath learning difficulties. And lo, there were in that region a great many swine, even more than people could number. And they beseech him saying, "Send the learning difficulties into the swine."

38

And he answered and said, "What do you take me for? Do you want to get me reported to the RSPCA?"

At that time they bring unto him one that was differently-abled. And behold he had compassion on him and saith, "Go, shew thyself to the Equal Access Officer and apply for a wheelchair ramp."

And behold there was a woman caught in adultery, in the very act. And he saith, "Lo, she doeth no wrong. Is it not good to take unto thyself many partners? For the former things have passed away. And what was un-swung is now swinging."

When they were in the region about Caesarea Philippi, he enquired of them, saying, "Whom do persons say that I am?"

And Simon Peter answereth, "Some say thou art John Lennon returned from the dead, and others say thou art El-vis."

And he turneth to Simon Peter and saith, "Whom say ye that I am?"

And Peter answered and said, "I haven't the foggiest. Every person must be free to make up his or her own mind: for behold, one opinion is a good as another."

The City Service

Think back to your schooldays. The end of term prize-giving. The hall full of the scent of polished oak and schoolboys. Young ladies don't smell of course, but only glow. The clump of shoes on wood as the staff mount the rostrum and the instant nostalgia of And Did Those Feet. The school prayer: cod-Cranmer from the late 19th century. Applause like light rain as the winners trudge across the stage to shake hands with the visiting worthy who will later speak worthily through the rising heat and intensifying aroma. Remember how the prize-winners strained not to look anything as un-cool as pleased with themselves. Then it's a moot point whether you hear the thud of the first pupil to faint before or after you inhale the stink of the first prize-winning fart. Soon, though it does not seem soon, cracked adolescent voices are croaking their way through I Vow to Thee My Country and you all pile out for lungsful of real air.

Well, the New Year City Service is just like the prize-giving ceremony – generally without the farts. It has been held in St Michael's every January for half a century, having been invented in the days when City men wore pinstripes and bowlers and carried brollies as they waddled penguin-like to their long lunches. Now City men have grown younger and become City persons; and the old uniform has been discarded in favour of the Armani suit, jazzy tie and mobile phone. The long lunch is gone too: nowadays the workaholics arrive at the office by seven in the morning and sit gazing into their computer screens for hours on end fortified only by capuccino or straight black from Starbucks or Coffee Republic. In the good old days – sorry, I mean the bad old sexist, old boy networked, colossal deals done over three hours at the chop-house to the accompaniment of large steaks, sticky toffee puddings, pints of claret and bushels of Taylor's Vintage days – there was a deceptive indolence at the office. Much work was done, but it was regarded as ungentlemanly to think of what went on as work. They weren't "City workers"; they were all, great or small, "Something in the City".

Nowadays, the fashionable youngsters aiming to make their first five million before burnout sit shirt-sleeved in front of their terminals and quit that position only for the loo or to step outside for a smoke break. In the old, unenlightened days when gentlemen were either Senior Service or Capstan Full Strength and passive smoking had not been discovered, everyone chain-smoked throughout the day in the oak-panelled offices. Old, un-tipped cigarette smoking City gents associated cocaine only with a trip to the dentist. Together with the cigarettes, the oak panelling has gone and the dealers sit in open-plan trading rooms as vast as football stadiums. The old gentlemen would have found it deafening, but such decibels are nothing to youngsters who spend their nights at clubs and discos.

The outdoor uniform of the new City person involves a black overcoat, usually worn open. To walk down Cheapside is to imagine you were at a series of posh funerals. They are on the mobile all the time. And, forbidden by the health police to smoke in the office, there is always a fag on the go. I once saw someone bethink himself just before he nearly put the mobile phone to his lips and the lighted cigarette in his ear. When in the street a mobile phone rings, the owner gives it all his attention, loses all sense of orientation and drifts around the pavement like a distressed ship. Or, as once happened to me, they stop dead and you have all on not to walk into the back of them. The women City persons wear black too, and they are groomed so expensively they look as if they are on their way to a posh and erotic funeral. The boys all dress alike and the girls all dress alike – odd for an age when there is so much talk of "individuality" and "self-expression".

Many of the old banks have closed and turned themselves into pubs. So in Cornhill, next to St Michael's, there is The Counting House and round the corner is a branch of the Wetherspoons chain, huge as a trading floor with the circular bar in the centre where the tellers used to stand. Sometimes in a drowsy reverie after a couple of glasses of the house white, you can half close your eyes and change the barmen and barmaids back into sober-suited bank clerks, counting out the pound notes in a swift silence. But there is no silence. Even in Wetherspoons, where they have banished musak, there is a constant roar of voices. They use their voices as a kind of gesticulation. They speak not so much to be heard as to be seen. Our oldest churchwarden, a City man in his day, called them "Hooray Henrys", but the voices are not as refined as that.

The talk is about clothes, celebs, clubbing, restaurants, soap operas and holidays in rare places. These holiday destinations come and go, in and out of fashion – just like the brand preferences for their mobile phones. Last year it was Vietnam. But colleagues would only turn up their noses if you said you were going to Vietnam this year. This year it's the Galapagos Islands – or is it the Great Wall of China? Skiing is forever – though Switzerland is passé. In place of the long lunch over claret in the chop-house, it's sushi, onion rings or something so slight it's nearly immaterial, accompanied by rocket salad and washed down with alcopops or diet coke. Everybody is on a diet all the time, though the talk about food is endless.

Their conversation is like constipation: sluggish, unmentionable. The subject-matter all empty-headedness, as if they spent their whole lives on the pages of a fashion mag. Yet they feel so superior. The sheer arrogance of ignorance: if you'd asked them an honest question about, say, Winston Churchill or carboniferous limestone, they would threaten to have you arrested for elitism and the violation of their human right to be thick. And then there is the accent and intonation: not only "fings" and "finks", which just might pass for the dregs of ancient Cockney, but the upward inflection at the end of every gobbet – a habit they have picked up from the Aussie soap operas. Given that and the toy-town jingles on their mobiles, what can anyone say except "O City, City!" and bewail a willed infantilism? They all have the bearing and, worse, one suspects, the aspirations of a twelve-year-old. The City has regressed to childhood.

The New Year City Service is held on the second Friday in January and it is my job to organise it. This means sending out three or four hundred invitations in December to chairmen of the big banks and insurance companies and to masters and clerks of the great Livery Companies. On the day, the church is full and there is a palpable atmosphere of nostalgia and intrigue: nostalgia for those old hymns and intrigue in anticipation that the distinguished visiting preacher might say something controversial or even indiscreet.

In my first year in the City, I was lucky to secure the oratorical talents of Miss Ann Widdecombe MP, who at the time was Shadow Home Secretary. Actually, she got me out of a hole because, having arrived at St Michael's only in November, I was desperately short of time in which to book a well-known speaker. Ann was the answer to a Rector's prayer, accepting my invitation by return post. When I sighed my relief down the telephone, her secretary said a trifle ecstatically, "You've managed to book the next Home Secretary, you know!" This was in the days when it was thought Ann was going to be something big in the government – perhaps even one day follow the iron lady herself into the top job.

I was surprised by her prettiness. She is not a figure who looks good on television, but in real life she has the fresh appearance of the classic 1950s' debutante. Her hair – well, in those days – was very black and her cheeks like white porcelain. But I'm getting ahead of myself. I mentioned her appearance, which is all very well – except she didn't appear. The service was due to begin at noon. The church packed. The organist navigating his way through the cheerfully labyrinthine counterpoint of Bach's New Year Pieces on our renowned instrument, first played by Henry Purcell in the 17th century. Five to twelve and the distinguished speaker had not arrived. I had a church warden go stand in Cornhill and look out to see that her official car did not drive past oblivious to our location. I perched myself on the top step and fretted, the pulse and nauseous adrenaline at top flight or fright level. Anxiety creeping through my flesh like the onset of a general anaesthetic. I felt stricken and it must have shown in my face to all the City folk scurrying by in the rain. I wore such a strained grimace that they might have taken me for a gargoyle.

Now and again I looked to my man in the street with desperate hopefulness. Surely Future Home Secretaries don't miss their appointments? The clock by the Royal Exchange sounded the hour gloomily and, as my church warden standing out in the middle of the street like a policeman on point duty – but a policeman in a surplice? - shook his head for the umpteenth time, I shrugged and went in to start the service. Everyone sang the lovely Epiphany opening hymn so cheerfully: Earth hath many a noble City. It seemed only to make matters worse. What when they discovered that the Rector had cocked it up – after all the confident publicity, too – and the Future Home Secretary didn't show up? I felt like a man going over the rapids. What would I do? Sick to the pit of my stomach, I tried to stop trembling in my stall and think straight. No doubt I could conjure up some sort of address myself based on the fading recollection of an old sermon. But they hadn't come to hear me: they had come – all three hundred of them – to hear the FHS.

The Master of the Worshipful Company of Drapers read his lesson and the Deputy Governor of the Bank of England read his. It was twenty past twelve and we were into the hymn before the address when I noticed a ghostly movement over towards the back of the south aisle. My man on point duty had entered the church and he was leading the tiny, unruffled figure of Miss Widdecombe gently to her place. It was like the arrival of the cavalry – but at nearly twenty-five minutes past high noon. She spoke about the Good Samaritan and said, "The rescuer of the man who fell among thieves told the innkeeper to look after the unfortunate and, on his return from his business trip, he would pay whatever extra expenses had been incurred. So you see, the whole message is about trust – a very pertinent lesson for us all in the City where a gentleman's word is his bond." The old City men looked up at her with something approaching adoration.

After the service we all strolled across the street to Drapers' Hall for the customary sumptuous reception. I felt something like the giddiness and euphoria Scrooge felt when he awoke on Christmas morning, after the visitation by the three spirits, and found he was still alive after all. Relief made me impetuous and I kissed the great lady on the cheek. She smiled the porcelain smile and said in her distinctively fractured intonation, "Sorry. Traffic." It didn't matter. Warmed by the festive haze in the glorious Drapers' Hall, it didn't matter at all.

The following year, the same curse struck again. This time our speaker was to be Frederick Forsyth, the thriller writer, an intelligently engaged political conservative. He arrived twenty-odd minutes late after the example of the FHS. No trouble with the traffic: he simply went to the wrong church. Frederick is well-known for his vigorous opposition to the EU bureaucracy. So after the choir had enjoyed an all cylinders firing rendition of Sir Hubert Parry's anthem I Was Glad, Frederick rose in the pulpit and began his address. It was memorable for the fact that he had learnt it by heart, word perfect. He told us how the members of the European Parliament stood earnestly airing their policies while the bureaucrats in the secretariat sat at the back listening and smiling sarcastically. "Then they proceeded to block or rewrite entirely the policies which the members had proposed."

Mentioning in passing his period spent as an observer in East Germany during the Cold War, he went on – as scornfully satirical as any Orwell or Koestler – to describe a hideous apparatus of control, of democracy being whatever the secretariat said it was; of commissars and apparatchiks; of rules designed to promote political stagnation. Then he said, "You must wonder why I am describing events that happened in a foreign country many years ago. I'm not. I'm describing the reality of Britain today." At this the congregation inhaled so sharply that I thought all the air would be drawn out of the church.

"Polite debates about whether Britain might lose its sovereignty by closer ties with the EU are all water under the bridge. We have lost our sovereignty already. Just read the Treaties of Maastricht and Amsterdam and there you will find the reality in the plain and oft-repeated statement that the aim of the EU is "ever closer political union".

What had started off as a coal and steel policy, become the European Common Market, then transmogrified without demur or democratic vote into first the European Economic Community, then the European Community and after that the European Union would soon raise itself into a European Superstate. In fact, in Frederick's view, it had virtually done so already.

This Ciceronian piece of oratory had the congregation mesmerised and, in the case of ninety eight per cent of them, in thrilled agreement.

The following year our speaker was Cardinal Archbishop Cormac Murphy-O'Connor – before he became engulfed by the scandal of paedophile priests in his Arundel Diocese. In fact, before he became a Cardinal. The Pope actually gave him his red hat the week after the New Year City Service so, when I wrote to thank him for his address, I said, "You see what comes from being select preacher at St Michael's!" Cormac – his personal origins bog Irish - began his sermon with a half-decent Irish story which put the audience in a good mood: "I was standing at a crossroads in Ireland last summer and there were two pubs opposite each other. I asked a passing local which one I should try for lunch. He replied, 'Well now, you see, if you go in one, you'll wish you'd gone in the other'." I can't remember anything else that he said in his drowsy brogue, but at least he had turned up on time and saved me from a heart attack.

It was a different atmosphere the following year when the philosopher Roger Scruton came. Slight, red-headed, he too arrived in good time and went straight to the back of the choir stalls to finish his sermon which turned out to be one of the most evocative I've ever heard: not preachy, not discursive at all, but full of *things*, full of landscapes and pastures and country churches and his old school – and schoolmasters who had befriended him. He said it was an elegy for the England we have lost:

"In these early English churches of flint and stone, a peculiar silence has been stored, along with the sweet, damp smell of plaster, the mouldering prayer books, the embroidered kneelers and the Victorian altar cloths with their gold and emerald fabrics, like robes left behind by some visiting angel... At the Communion, the organist would improvise on muted pipes, whimsical, watery sequences, full of fifths and fourths in the manner of Vaughan Williams or Herbert Howells. It was as though the Holy Ghost himself were present, humming quietly to himself in an English accent...God, as represented in the sacred texts and liturgy of the Church of England, was an Englishman, uncomfortable in the presence of enthusiasm, reluctant to make a fuss, but trapped into making public speeches. God hid his discomfiture behind a solemn screen of words, using old-fashioned idioms which somehow excused the severity of what He was bound by His office to say."

The shyness and diffidence of his delivery and manner, the sparseness of his physical frame and the gentle tenor of the way he uttered these truths gave to his performance an extraordinary power and authority. It is rare that one is able to describe a sermon as thrilling. A retired parson said to me as we crossed Cornhill on our way to Drapers' Hall, "He speaks with authority – not as the Scribes."

What is an Archbishop for?

There were all sorts of rumours in circulation about what Dr Rowan Williams might do when he established his reign over us as Archbishop of Canterbury. Some evangelical traditionalists fear that he will agree to ordain active homosexuals. Is that a problem? Personally, I don't care what people do in their private lives so long as it doesn't frighten the horses. What is objectionable, however, is proselytisation of a particular lifestyle as if it were a Golden Rule. I thought when homosexual acts between consenting adults in private were permitted back in the 1960s that this was a humane lifting of an intolerable burden on a minority. But what has happened in the intervening years is that discreet private associations have been made a matter of politics. Homosexuals in the 21st century don't ask simply for toleration, but approval. And they insist on the right to perform in public sexual acts for which traditional married couples would be prosecuted. As someone said forty years ago, "I hear they've made homosexuality legal. I'm leaving the country before they make it compulsory." "Gay Pride" marches through central London indecently proclaim to all and sundry what ought – and always used to be, even among heterosexuals – the most private acts in the bedroom. The love that dare not speak its name now shrieks intolerantly from the housetops.

Others suspect that Dr Williams will want to disestablish the Church – that is break the historic link between Church and State by which the Monarch is Supreme Governor of the Church of England. The man in the street is bored by this issue. He thinks – if he regards the issue at all – that "disestablishmentarianism" is nothing more than a contender for the longest word in the English language. The point is rather that the establishment of the Church is one of the most democratic aspects of our constitution: in Hooker's words, it means simply, "Every man of England a member of the Church of England" – with no further religious or political tests. You can't get more liberal than that. To disestablish the Church, which is Williams' reported desire, would be to abolish the easy-going political-religious settlement under which we have prospered for four hundred years and replace it with a politically correct arrangement under which everyone claiming to be a member of the Church of England would have to declare upon what that claim was based: one imagines, "I go to Family Knees Up three weeks out of the four and I despise the Book of Common Prayer." In effect, the act of disestablishment would turn the all-inclusive Church into a sect for the like-minded – if "mind" may be said to play any part in these discussions.

In normal times, these topics would loom like battleships and be huge issues of public debate. But since the destruction of the Twin Towers, times are not normal: the western world is under threat and our civilisation is in the severest danger it has been in since the end of the Cold War. In the face of this threat, what really frightens me is the new Archbishop's attitude to the war on Islamic terrorism. Dr Williams was in New York at a conference on 11th September. He has given us his reflections on the atrocities and their aftermath in his booklet Writing in the Dust.

Dr Williams thinks that the West should not retaliate: "If I decide to answer in the same terms, that is how the conversation will continue." There is a confusion here between revenge and justice. While I may seek on my own behalf to follow the teaching of Christ to turn the other cheek, I must not do this on behalf of those who have suffered innocently. It is my duty to take up the sword on behalf of the fatherless children and the widow. Not to do this is to concede victory to the aggressors, and that would be unjust. Would Dr Williams argue that the brave men who fought back against the terrorists in the fourth plane were wrong to do so? If they had not summoned up oceans of courage and attacked the terrorists, then almost certainly the fourth plane would have been deliberately crashed into a densely populated target and the loss of life would have been catastrophically greater.

Dr Williams will not even allow us to describe the terrorists as evil men: "Bombast about evil individuals doesn't help in understanding anything." Well, of course, bombast about anything is pretty futile; but there is a world of difference between bombast and the true judgement that lets us see evil for what it is. The Archbishop wants to "understand" the terrorists' motivation. He reckons they had no choice: "We have something of the freedom to consider whether or not we turn to violence and so, in virtue of that very fact, are rather different from those who experience their world as leaving no other option." This is a high-grade sample of the drivel we have heard these last three years from those in the west who despise the civilisation which is their inheritance. Of course the suicide bombers had "other options": not every impoverished Muslim thinks that the only answer to his problems is to destroy New York.

Once we have admitted that the atrocity was not the terrorists' fault, what next? "We begin to find some sense of what they and we might together recognise as good". Really? But it is impossible to make common moral cause between democratic freedom and the rule of law on the one hand and psychopathic, nihilistic killing on the other. How would we begin to do such a thing? Do sit down, Osama, pour yourself another lemonade and let's discuss globalisation.

Next, Dr Williams proceeds to rubbish the war on terrorism as "a discharge of tension". And he asks, "What possible guarantee could there be that the abolition of terrorism had been achieved?" Well, of course, in historical matters there are no guarantees, as there are no inevitabilities – unless you're a Marxist. But that is quite different from saying that the war is accomplishing nothing. America's firm military response has already convinced other rogue states – Sudan and Yemen, for example - that harbouring terrorists is no longer in their national interest. And it has persuaded Libya to renounce its WMD programme. Dr Williams' rhetoric excites him to conclusions which are plain perversions of the truth: "We conspicuously don't have an alternative for the future of Afghanistan." This is nonsense in the face of the facts that the beginnings of decent government in the country have been established, and every day brings news of fresh millions in aid and investment to rebuild its infrastructure.

It is at this point that Dr Williams' misapprehensions descend into irritable fantasy. He says that the bombing campaign in Afghanistan "...assaulted public morale by allowing random killing as a matter of calculated policy". That is simply not true. The coalition gave the Taliban scores of warnings before the bombing started, and took great pains to avoid civilian casualties.

Dr Williams merely repeats the old story again of the nasty capitalists' exploitation of the Third World's picturesque poor. He says: "We could ask whether the further destabilising of a massively resentful Muslim world were really unavoidable." Should petulance and resentment be rewarded then? What, when these emotions result in terrorist atrocities?

Dr Williams' fantasy turns out to be a paranoid one: "Every transaction in the developed economies of the West can be interpreted as an act of aggression against the economic losers in the worldwide game." Well it could be interpreted in that way, but it would be a false interpretation. The fact is that many of those Third World countries which have decided to hitch their economic wagon to the western engine are raising the living standards of their people. Paranoia usually goes hand in hand with sentimentality, and we find buckets of the stuff here: "As we protest at how the West is hated, how we never meant to oppress or diminish other cultures, how we never intended to undermine Islamic integrity, we must try not to avoid the pain of grasping that we are not believed."

Dr Williams' conclusion is the complete inversion of the truth: "It is hard to start any sort of conversation when your conversation partner believes, in all sincerity, that your aim is to silence them." So Muslim terrorists are our conversation partners are they! But it was these "conversation partners" who successfully silenced more than 3000 of us in New York on 11th September. One thing above all else puzzles me. Tony Blair, to his credit, has taken an extremely firm line against the terrorists and in his support for George W. Bush. The Prime Minister appointed Dr Williams to the Canterbury Archbishopric. Didn't he read Writing in the Dust first?

Dr Williams has been praised all over the newspapers as a man who excites us to awe and affection. He was even described here and there as a saint. In fact, as his writings reveal, he is an old-fashioned class warrior. He dislikes our way of life in the West and romanticises the Islamic world quite as much as the old Marxist fellow-travellers used to romanticise the Soviet Union. As I say, this wouldn't matter much in normal times, but these days we are living on the edge of destruction. I should like to remind the Archbishop of Canterbury of the World War II slogan, "Careless talk costs lives".

The Golden Jubilee

Our ceremonials – and fun and games – for the Queen's Golden Jubilee were a sensation. I went round early with the begging bowl and Fuller's Brewery was generous enough almost to drown us in ale: two hundred and fifty cans to make us think twice about St Paul's strictures on "riotings and drunkenness". At least we got through the celebrations without, I think, falling into that other part of the sinful trap which the Apostle warns against: "chambering and wantonness".

We put on a festival Eucharist – Mozart, The Coronation Mass – and I thought back to the June day in 1953 when the Queen was crowned sixteen months after that yellow, lowering day in February when her father the old King died. Her Majesty was crowned in the same week that Hillary and Tenzing were the first to climb Everest, and the country bubbled along in cheerful rejoicing fit to be set to music, to one of Handel's anthems. Indeed, the greatest of those royal anthems was played for her Coronation: Zadok the priest and Nathan the prophet anointed Solomon King...

It poured all day on 2nd June 1953, but 2nd June 2002 poured sunshine like warm honey over the whole land. We were well-stocked with wine and everyone pillaged their larder to bring enough to feed more than the proverbial five thousand. One of our old soldiers ran the barbecue with regimental dignity and a swift efficiency worthy of the SAS. There had been so much republican knocking copy in the broadsheets that I decided to preach a loyal sermon.

"In 1928, Winston Churchill visited Balmoral and saw the two-year-old Princess Elizabeth for the first time. He wrote to his wife: 'She is a character. She has an air of authority and reflectiveness astonishing in an infant.' A year or so later, Sir Owen Morshead told of an incident at Windsor. The officer commanding the guard strode across to where the pram stood and said, 'Permission to march off, please, Ma'am?' There was the inclination of a bonneted head and a wave from a tiny paw.

"The Queen has often deployed her ready wit, especially to defuse embarrassing occasions. Once when she was in a tea-shop near

51

Sandringham, a woman leaned forward and said, 'Excuse me, but you do look awfully like the Queen.' The Queen replied, 'How very reassuring!' Again, at a banquet she was served with asparagus and her neighbour at the table watched her to see how she would deal with the stout, buttery, home-grown stems. When he came to be served, the Queen turned to him and said, 'Good. Now it's my turn to see you make a pig of yourself!'

"On another occasion, the Queen's coach splashed mud over a pedestrian in Sandringham. The pedestrian, a woman, shouted something and the Queen answered her, 'I quite agree.' The Duke of Edinburgh turned to the Queen and asked, 'What did she say, dear?' The Queen replied, 'Bastards!'

"Much later, at a public ceremony, Mrs Thatcher felt embarrassed because she'd turned up in an outfit which closely resembled the Queen's. Afterwards, Downing Street discreetly asked the palace whether there was any way by which in future the Prime Minister might know in advance what Her Majesty intended to wear. The palace phoned back with a message directly from the Queen: 'Do not worry. The Queen does not notice what other people are wearing.'

"The levellers, following Walter Bagehot, try to persuade us to regard the dignified aspects of our Constitution as outmoded habits of mind which belonged to the bad old days before, in a plethora of ludicrous and unworkable charters, we were urged to replace our traditional understanding of ourselves as subjects with the alien and republican term citizens. There are many who would reduce the Royal Family and make the remnant of them abandon the state coach and take to bicycles. Polly Toynbee has written that the Queen should move out of Buckingham Palace and into a council house. I won't suggest where Ms Toynbee should go and live.

"And now, this week, a New Labour think tank – surely an oxymoron? - says that a useful role for the monarchy would be to travel round the world apologising for the sins of the empire. They say future monarchs should be educated at comprehensive schools – like what they are. And even their grudging support for the retention of a little royal ceremonial is only out of the pig philosophy that says it's good for the tourist industry.

"But ceremonial is not useless trimming. Things cannot be adequately replaced by mere thoughts. Because we are bodies as well as minds, we need the externals. Appearances are themselves part of the reality they point to. This is the sacramental way of being. I'm sure you remember from the days of your Confirmation classes that a sacrament is an outward and visible sign of an inward and spiritual grace. The Orb, the Sceptre and the Crown embody what they represent. The Coronation Service is sacramental, complete with holy oil. There is a nice remark by the poet Robert Graves, who met the Queen not long after her Coronation. He said: 'The holy oil has taken for that girl: it worked for her all right.'

"Some will say that in the modern world the Queen does not rule. They are mistaken. The Queen rules through her ministers just as the ministers govern through their civil servants – or, at least, they used to before the coming of the likes of Jo Moore. Of course, the minister does not attend to every small item of business. It is his job to secure the coherence of his department. It is the Queen's function to secure the coherence of the realm. T.S. Eliot wrote in 1939: 'You cannot expect continuity and coherence in politics, you cannot expect reliable behaviour on fixed principles persisting through changed situations, unless there is an underlying political philosophy: not of a party, but of the nation.' The Queen is the centre and guarantee of the nation; its embodiment.

"Having defaced and deformed institutions such as Parliament, the Church, the law and the university, the modernisers, in a fit of hysterical self-hatred, egged on by ignorant, envious and sensationalising sections of the mass media, recently turned their destructive spite on the monarchy which too will have to be modernised - after the style of the Queen's having being forced into a nauseating, sentimental linking of arms in that other temple to the modernisers' failure, the Dome. We know not what we do: for the monarchy is the living symbol of the nation. Any lack of esteem for it is the outward and visible sign of self-contempt. We need to value something. And what you value shows you what you're worth. People will revere something: better a thousand-year-old monarchy than Posh Spice, Beckham and Kylie. The marvellous tide of respect shown by the people following the death of the Queen Mother has demonstrated vigorously that the majority in Britain still prefer Rule Britannia to Cool Britannia.

53

"We have been here before. In the 17th century the monarchy was abolished and the country was governed for eleven years by a puritanical, politically-correct dictatorship until the Cromwellian totalitarianism was shown up for what it was and we got our king back. The cries at the time of Cromwell were eerily similar to what we are hearing today: the need to 'modernise' - think of the New Model Army - and so destroy the traditional institutions which had served the country well for centuries. Even a bad king is better than a so-called 'Lord Protector' who in reality was a dictator. Cromwell abolished Parliament. There are those today who would do similarly by by-passing it at every opportunity and governing instead by a close circle of cronies and a horde of un-elected advisors. Where's the democracy in that?

"By contrast, Her Majesty has served this country with distinction and self-sacrifice for fifty years. Every day she gives us a living example of what love of country means. Long may she reign. God bless her!"

There was no mistaking where St Michael's congregation of the faithful, the livery and leading City men stood: they greeted the close of my address with a loud round of applause.

It was wonderful to see millions turn out to express their love and gratitude to the Queen; and to see off all those media prophecies about the monarchy as doomed. It was the left-wing press that was doomed, as the crowds lined the Mall in their hundreds of thousands. Of course, the usual suspects in the Church of England did perform their customary spoiling act. For example, Church Times gave half a page to Rev'd Dr Kenneth Leech who used the space to write: "Monarchy is opposed to the Christian tradition of equality." He referred to Her Majesty as "...that child of God whom some people call the Queen." Some people? What does Dr Leech suggest we call her? He says, "The Jubilee stands for the preservation of inequality, privilege and injustice."

Shame on the Editor of Church Times for letting this class warrior, this East End apparatchik, loose at a time of national rejoicing. His article drips with malice and hatred: "At every point, monarchy is opposed to the Christian tradition of equality and solidarity". Not in the Christian tradition in which I was brought up – the same in which St Peter urges, "Fear God. Honour the King" (I Peter 2: 17); in which the

Sovereign is Defender of the Faith and Supreme Governor of the Church; and in which the Monarch, in the Royal Declaration annexed to The Book of Common Prayer, says, "We hold it most agreeable to this our kingly office and our own religious zeal to conserve and maintain the Church committed to our charge." Or Article 37 of The Thirty-nine Articles where it says, "The King's majesty hath the chief power in this realm of England of all estates of the realm whether they be ecclesiastical or civil."

Leech asks us to pity him and his cronies: "In 1974 a small group of eight socialist Anglican Catholics met at St Matthew's, Bethnal Green. We felt isolated in the Church because we were on the Left." This must be some sort of sick joke. Now that the Berlin Wall has come down, there are more Lefties in the General Synod than there are in Russia. It is they and their socialist policies that have ruled the Church for thirty years – or would Leech have us believe that it was the Tory Party at Prayer which supported unilateral nuclear disarmament, the miners' strike and which devised the Marxist policy document Faith in the City back in the 1980s? The General Synod, and particularly its Board for Social Responsibility, is dominated by socialists and collectivists who constantly produce biased and unrepresentative reports on everything from glue-sniffing to overseas aid.

The government of the Church of England is consumed by the politics of envy. What other explanation can there be for the malevolent Puritanism that orders bishops to give up their chauffeurs and their claret, to vacate their already modest palaces and take up residence among the lumpen proletariat? Of course Our Lord loved the poor, but there are scores of accounts in the gospels of his agreeable feasts among the rich. The truth is that Christianity is an incarnational religion, and this means that whenever the Church's status and physical presence is reduced there will inevitably follow a decline in its influence.

The Synod is full of talkative politicos who hate the traditional dignity of the national church: this is why they seek disestablishment (and they will get it under Blair and Rowan Williams); why they sneer at any appearance of the old image of the bishop as a prince in his church. This obsession with egalitarianism is only a thinly-disguised covetousness. It is the continuation of the spiteful class warfare of the last century. What are these levellers except the provisional wing of Old Labour - ecclesiastical branch?

By contrast, we rejoiced to Mozart and Handel, stuffed ourselves at the barbecue and washed the lot down with Fuller's good ale as we sang all three verses of the National Anthem, including the one that goes,

> O Lord our God arise,
> Scatter her enemies
> And make them fall.
> Confound their politics,
> Frustrate their knavish tricks,
> On thee our hopes are fixed,
> God save us all!

As someone remarked as we sat drowsily in the afternoon sunshine: "And if anyone thinks the Queen has no enemies – let them look no further than the corridors of the BBC."

Some Funerals are Funnier than Others

I walk up Cheapside after the Friday lunchtime Holy Communion at St Michael's and call in Tesco's as usual to get some weekend shopping. I know all the boys and girls on the checkouts – and a fine cosmopolitan bunch they are. This is what good race relations are about, if you ask me: not ludicrous and contradictory declarations such as that found in the compendium of illiteracy and illogic called the MacPherson Report, which idiotically claims that "...a racist incident is anything that the victim, or any other person, says it is". This is the language of the looking glass or the tower of Babel. It would involve, for instance, the bizarre outcome that, should I invite you to have a cup of tea, you might with perfect sanity interpret my invitation as a racist incident and shop me to the magistrate. This is an example of where political correctness is not just plain silly but evil, because it is destructive of good social relationships: presenting as it does the archetype of race relations on the model of everyone bearing a grudge against everyone else.

But the boys and the girls on the checkouts – devout Moslems, chuckling Hindus and ribald West Indians – and of course I am aware that I have probably committed an unpardonable offence against acceptable race politics just by writing the first half of this current sentence - treat me with an affectionate mercilessness: "You'll be going to bed for the afternoon when you've drunk that bottle of wine, Father?"

"All you have to do is turn up at livery dinners and posh weddings, eh?"

One hears in the background hush the acid indigestion accent of Esmeralda Salmonella. I try to give as good as I get: "Why don't you go back to where you come from?"

"Sure, Father, I will. I'm on the tube to Clapham every night." And yet another cherry blossom smile.

She relents and says with her huge brown eyes and tenderness in her voice, "No, I'm sorry. You have to bury people, don't you – do funerals, and that?"

"Yes, but it's not all misery, you know. There is such a thing as Christian hope. And then sometimes funny things happen at funerals." And I began to tell her about Jason's dad...

Jason was a City insurance underwriter. He used to come to St Michael's every Friday for the lunchtime Holy Communion. His mother had died and Jason lived with his old dad, a former merchant seaman and "a rambunctious old bugger", in Jason's own words. Dad was religious in the sense that he kept regular observances. He went to his wife's grave every morning and sat there for a while, had a smoke and from there went on to the pub where he had six pints and three glasses of whisky. Then home to cook Jason's supper.

His bronchitis, always a trouble to him, got worse and, after a mercifully short period of distressing illness, he died. Jason wanted to do things right for the old man, so he hired a coach and horses and decorated the cortege with ostrich feathers and the coffin with the Red Ensign in honour of his Merchant Navy days. We made off to the church like a moving scene out of Dickens – making sure that the coach passed the pub where he had for so long and with such diligence turned up for his lunchtime boozing.

The procession stopped at another of the hostelries which the old man had frequented over many years. Jason had promised his dad that the cortege would make a formal halt there. The old man was duly laid out in state in the four ale bar, his usual pint on top of the coffin. A toast was proposed, his health drunk and, as they say, there was not a dry eye in the house.

The church service was a simple family affair – heartfelt, with unpretentious little speeches from the family and clergy, including a very amusing one from Jason himself. Then it was off across the road to the cemetery. It was a brilliant blue and golden January day and there was still frost on the ground at one o'clock. We meandered to the graveside and began the words of committal. The praying finished, the undertaker's men stepped forward to lower the coffin into the ground. Embarrassingly, the coffin would not go into the hole. It was stuck. They angled and shoved and grunted and grimaced, but still it would not go in. By some mischance or miscalculation, the grave had not been dug to the right size.

Nothing for it, then, but for one of the men to take off his frock coat

– to reveal a T-shirt with a skull and crossbones on the back and a slogan on the front that was rude enough to discomfit everyone, except perhaps the poor old bugger who was trying to get safely into his last resting-place – and start to dig. Now digging graves is hard enough at the best of times, but trying to shift frosty earth requires the strength of Hercules and the patience of Job. Twenty minutes later and after three more attempts to get the old man to rest, the substantial congregation were obviously bemused and embarrassed. It was then that Jason relieved the tension by calling out in a loud and cheerful voice, "Ah well, dad, y'old bugger – you were always tight [he meant tipsy, not stingy] when you were alive, and now you're too tight to fit in your own grave!"

It seemed to do the trick. One more heave and dad slid into his neat little portion of winter earth and the rest of us went off to his local and spent the afternoon in gleeful recollection of the manner of his departing.

In recent years, cremation has become much more – let me try to find the right word – popular. It presents a vast cultural change from the days of the family undertaker and all the intimate qualities which used to accompany a death in the parish. The emotional shift is profound. The culture that met death with an aspidistra in the front room where the corpse was laid out to be visited by friends and relations has given way to the arrangement whereby the body is removed while it is still warm and deposited in that euphemism called the Chapel of Rest, and thence to the crematorium.

The crematorium is a weird mixture of nonconformist chapel and small local theatre. It has to be fairly bland since it is required to provide funeral rites for all sorts and conditions of people of all religions and none. This guarantees that the interior must be rather nondescript: for a secular Jew, for example, would not expect to enjoy his funeral surrounded by crosses and stained glass windows in honour of the Virgin Mary and the rest of the trappings of High Anglicanism. There is therefore a pervasive sense of utility rather than ornament – which is perhaps fitting for a method of disposal which is still regarded as "modern" and "scientific". But it is possible for crematoria to witness to tastefulness and so, to take one example, the crematorium at London's Golders Green is a very attractive and spiritually appropriate building. The gardens are spacious and serene and the cloisters, paved with memorial stones, are as fine as any you will find in a cathedral.

Both Ralph Vaughan Williams, the composer who used to conduct our St Michael's Singers before the Second World War, and Harold Darke, who was our organist for fifty years, were cremated at Golders Green. There is a fascinating atmosphere of Edwardian commercial sense about this place which displays in its century-old waiting-room advertisements for "services to suit all denominations" and which, in keeping with the tone of high modernity, also assure us of "cleanliness, purity and economy". But I have a tale to tell of one crematorium – not Golders Green – which might make some people prefer the old-fashioned burial after all.

This was a comic-macabre event in which I can claim entire innocence. Still, there's no smoke without fire – no, not even in the municipal crematorium. I set off to conduct the funeral of Harry Adams who had died, aged eighty-one. "A dear husband, dad and grandad," proclaimed the largest wreath. Another said, "From all at the Packhorse and Mule." As luck and the metropolitan traffic would have it, I arrived early and so I had time to pay a pastoral visit on the men who operated the furnaces "in the kitchen" as they were wont to say. Brothers they were, not twins but much alike; small, bony creatures in their black cassocks, they looked like undernourished crows.

I said, "Good morning, boys. Did you get your pay rise?"

"Oh yes, sir: we've money to burn now!" As he said this, he pushed a button and a quiet whirring came from behind one of the furnaces. The other scrawny assistant called out, "Come and look at the new calcium remains machine, Father." (He pronounced the "i" in "calcium" like the "y" in "dye") "See, it's like a spin-dryer. You put your calcium remains in..."

"My calcium remains?"

"Well, you know what I mean – his calcium remains, hers; you know..."

He went on eagerly as if trying to sell me one of the machines for my home use: "You put calcium remains in and shut the lid. Then some stone balls belt about like crazy until all the remains are done into a fine powder." He enjoyed this. He pulled down the lid and a ferocious din arose from the tall, cylindrical machine. He grinned a grin of demonic triumph. Then the other assistant reappeared, grimacing and gesticulating above the noise. His mate stopped the hurtling stone balls so he could hear his colleague's message: "They're here!"

The hearse passed slowly through the main entrance and along the wooded drive. A glorious day, all cherry blossom and birdsong. The sunlight gleamed on the quiet and quality car as it pulled up outside the oak-panelled door of the chapel. Half a dozen saloon cars drew up just behind. Frail old Enid Adams all in black, with a black veil and a bunch of yellow flowers in her hands, stepped unsteadily out of the first car. Derrington the undertaker smiled gently as he took her hand. I was in my place with the Prayer Book open at the right page. The computerised musak played a sugary introit and the people sat down. The chapel was warm, filled with dusty sunlight and the whole event went beautifully until the very end.

In that particular crematorium, there was a quaint, Gothic mechanism – a partition in the wall behind the bier. It was more or less circular, and designed so that when the parson pushed the button marked "Blessing" on his lectern at the end of the service, the partition slowly opened, the woodwork dividing into six pieces like petals falling from a flower. At the same time, the top part of the bier began to move forward and slide gently into the gap in the wall. Finally, a curtain closed behind the coffin and the effect was thus generated among the mourners that the dear departed had passed smoothly to his final resting-place; whereas the assistants in the furnace-room knew that it was only his penultimate resting place – a trolley placed discreetly behind the partition in order to receive the coffin. A trolley usually placed there. A trolley almost always placed there…but not this time, alas!

There was something wrong with the moving part of the bier. So, when I pressed the "Blessing" button, instead of a slow, smooth movement of the coffin, it lurched forward with a loud, metallic "Chung!" and frightened the mourners. Those from the Packhorse and Mule were no doubt wondering if Harry had decided to come back for "last orders". The coffin dived through the gaping partition, and there followed an enormous crash from what I suppose we should refer to as "the other side". There followed two yelled words from the other side – the second of which was "hell!". Charlie Martin in the front pew looked up, startled out of his wits, and thinking, no doubt, that he had just heard old Harry's first comment on the quality of the afterlife.

I tried to look cool as an iceberg. I walked out from behind the lectern and stood at the front of the nave from where I quietly asked the mourners to stay in their places for a moment. Then, while they waited, I slipped through the side door into the furnace-room and returned in an instant to say casually, "All's well. A bad fault in the air-conditioning, that's all." I think we got away with it.

But some funerals you never get used to. One Friday, I arrived home just after two o'clock to find the front room in the Rectory full of strangers. Father, mother, grandmother, siblings, uncles and aunts: it had all the marks of irretrievable sadness and distress. Nobody was saying anything. No one moved. They all looked as if they had been glued to their chairs. My wife had distributed cups of tea, and now the cups were empty. They had been waiting to ask something of me.

"Our little Alice," the mother began, "was not expected to be delivered alive. But she was. Then they told us she could die any minute. But she didn't die. She gathered strength and lived for six weeks. We saw her smile. And her warm little hand closed up in mine. Then she did die. We've come to ask you if you will do the funeral."

And the eyes look up, beseeching, sorrowful beyond description. And ridiculously guilty – as if the mother had willed the death of her first-born; as if she could have done anything about it. But the tragedies of the children are visited upon the parents.

They brought the white coffin on the day – a bright blue autumn day, dry with rattling leaves in the church porch. Dry leaves, I thought, as I stood there waiting for the hearse, which were in their own day moist and soft. Surely the new shoots are but the grandchildren of those who have gone before? Vacuous conjecture. But what else might occupy the mind while one awaits the coming of a little one who departed almost before she arrived? The mind wrestling to save itself with mouse-like displacement activity – as when that little creature, oppressed by the cat, takes leave (no doubt to the sullen cat's amazement) to wash his face and paws.

As it happens, the Church has all the forces necessary to cope with these derelictions: except of course there are no such forces except the blatant, despairing affirmation of hope in the face of rank despair. Here comes an undertaker carrying a tiny white coffin. He places it not on the usual trestle but on a rocking-horse. It seems bizarre, a pretend funeral, a child's game. Disney-macabre. The mother and father hardly able to move for grief. And yet what emerges from their lips is, "I believe in the resurrection of the dead and the life of the world to come."

The choir, normally boisterous, irreverent, full of the Mozartian scatological banter, fallen silent: sitting, robed early, in the vestry sipping their mineral water from their plastic bottles and pretending to study the harmony in Walford Davies' God be in my head...

God be at mine end, and at my departing...

The little baby had barely arrived before she was bidden to depart. The mother and father look up and the priest feels suddenly bankrupt: not because he doesn't believe the gospel of resurrection – he does, and here believes it more strongly than ever – but because in this extremity the resurrection is being tested to destruction.

"Like as the father pitieth his own children... in the midst of life we are in death... of whom may we seek for succour but of thee, O Lord, who for our sins art justly displeased... yet O Lord most holy, O Lord most mighty, suffer us not at our last hour, for any pains of death to fall from thee...Write, blessed are the dead for they rest from their labours..."

What labours in a child only six weeks old?

Dies illa, dies irae, calamitatis et miseriae, dies magna et amara valde...

There is a Christian tradition and this is all we have in these bleak hours. I took up Dostoevsky's The Brothers Karamazov and read:

"Listen mother," said the elder. "Once in olden times a holy saint saw in the temple a mother like you weeping for her little one, whom God had taken. 'Knowest thou not,' said the saint to her, 'how bold these little ones are before the throne of God? Verily there are none bolder than they in the kingdom of Heaven. "Thou didst give us life, O Lord," they say, "and scarcely had we looked upon it when Thou didst take it back again."'

And so boldly they ask and ask again that God gives them at once the rank of angels. 'Therefore,' said the saint, 'thou, too, O mother , rejoice and weep not, for thy little son is with the Lord in the fellowship of the angels.'

That's what the saint said to the weeping mother of old. He was a great saint and he could not have spoken falsely. Therefore you, too, mother know that your little one is surely before the throne of God, is rejoicing and happy, and praying to God for you. Therefore, weep, but rejoice."

The woman listened to him, looking down with her cheek in her hand. She sighed deeply:

"My Nikita tried to comfort me with the same words as you. 'Foolish one,' he said, 'Why weep? Our son is no doubt singing with the angels before God.' He says that to me, but he weeps himself. I see that he cries like me. 'I know, Nikita,' said I. 'Where could he be if not with the Lord God? Only, here with us now he's not as he used to sit beside us before. And if only I could look upon him one little time, if only I could peep at him one little time, without going up to him, without speaking, if I could be hidden in a corner and only see him for one little minute, hear him playing in the yard, calling in his little voice, 'Mammy, where art thou?'

If only I could hear him pattering with his little feet about the room just once, only once; for so often, so often how I remember he used to run to me and shout and laugh, if only I could hear his little feet I should know him. But he's gone. Father, he's gone, and I shall never hear him again. Here's his little sash, but him I shall never see or hear now."

She drew out of her bosom her boy's little embroidered sash, and as soon as she looked at it she began shaking with sobs, hiding her eyes with her fingers, through which the tears flowed in a sudden stream.

"It is Rachel of old," said the elder, "weeping for her children, and will not be comforted because they are not. Such is the lot set on earth for you mothers. Be not comforted. Consolation is not what you need. Weep and be not consoled, but weep. Only every time you weep, be sure to remember that your little one is one of the angels of God, that he looks down from there at you and sees you and rejoices at your tears, and points at them to the Lord God; and a long while yet will ye keep that great mother's grief. But it will turn in the end to quiet joy, and your bitter tears will be only tears of tender sorrow that purifies the heart and delivers it from sin. And I shall pray for the repose of your child's soul. What was his name?"

And then the soaring soprano solo, the Schubert Ave Maria – into the hands of our Blessed Mother. Into the hands of her father who stooped to pick up the coffin from the white rocking-horse. Moving in a slow march. His face a mask of bland concentration. I turned and led the heartbroken procession to the church porch where the dry leaves still whirled and crackled, and the sun poured its misty light over the old stones:

May the angels lead thee into paradise: may the martyrs receive thee at thy coming, and lead thee into the holy city of Jerusalem. May the choir of angels receive thee, and mayest thou have eternal rest with Lazarus, who once was poor.

Livery or Liverish?

There are now a hundred and two City of London Livery Companies, most of them medieval trades guilds such as the Drapers, Merchant Taylors and Goldsmiths: though modern companies have been added to the list – such as the Hackney Carriage Drivers and the cybernetic Information Technologists. Most of the liverymen of these companies are "speculative" rather than "operative". I mean, I don't think there are any drapers in the Drapers' Company or any Merchant Taylors among the Merchant Taylors. Exceptions are found in the Guild of Air Pilots and Air Navigators and the Honourable Company of Master Mariners, whose members are all hands-on practitioners of those professions.

It has to be said that not all livery dinners are equally relaxed. The companies have their different characteristics and ethos. The Air Pilots and Navigators and the Honourable Company of Master Mariners are men's men who enjoy a bit of racy banter. Other companies are rather more reserved and lean towards formality. I wouldn't dream of trying on at, say, the Merchant Taylors or the Mercers the sort of stuff I can get away with among the airmen and sailors. This is not to say that the more formal gatherings are dowdy or the members Grundyish; it is just a case of a different ethos and you learn to feel your way towards what's appropriate and what isn't. I mean, you wouldn't tell those jokes about the adventures of young ladies from various parts of the country at a gala dinner attended by the Queen – though such tales were told with alacrity at the RAF Club do in the presence of Prince Philip.

Just now and again, though, there is a slight tendency towards mild pomposity and the tedious spectacle of men taking themselves just a bit too seriously. I was honoured to be asked to become Chaplain to one of the Companies for whom my first duty was to say Grace at their annual banquet. I wanted to try to catch something of the gist, the essence of the administrator, so I said,

> With reference to yours of 22nd,
> We accept this feast to which we're beckoned,
> To give thanks for fellowship and food

To the Maker and Preserver of all that's good:
We are much obliged that our thanks are heard –
Signed, yours faithfully, Secretary Bird.

I imagined there was nothing too blasphemous in such an invocation. In fact, as soon as I had finished speaking, there was an outburst of laughter and a round of applause. The ordinary mortal might at this point be reasonably expected to think that his words had been found agreeable to the assembled diners. I confess, I sat down to the banquet quietly pleased with the response to what I'd said. The salmon, duck and wines were excellent and the rest of the evening passed splendidly.

Some months later, I received a phone call from the Master of the Company to request that I should say Grace again at the next annual banquet. "But," he cautioned, "we don't expect any levity to intrude. After your last Grace, two Past Masters objected strongly to the light-hearted note that had crept in." But it hadn't "crept in" – it was deliberate, on the assumption that our lot in this world is not to mope about intensifying the oppression of misery, but actually to enjoy laughter and company: or else what are livery companies for? So what should I say at the next banquet...

Remove from our hearts, O Lord, every tincture of levity;
Let joy be not so much mentioned among us:
Deliver us, we beseech thee, from all merriment,
And cast us into that superior gloom
So beloved of Past Masters.

In the end, I hadn't the courage and instead said a long Latin Grace – a scurrilous one, far more objectionable than my own effort of the year before. It was received with a solemn chorus of "Amen". Ironic, actually, because the Latin Grace was a lot less decorous than the one by which I was originally adjudged to be so at fault.

But don't run away with the idea that the great Companies are all stuffy and strait-laced. Hospitality and riotous socialising have always been a big part of the livery scene. Sometimes more so than others. In 1585, the Cutlers accounts showed forty-four official visits to taverns and inns "for making various precepts, including one for a lottery". Occasionally these could get out of hand – as when a liveryman, Mr Tedcastle, was fined eight pence "for speaking indecent words in St George's Fields". In Elizabethan times, the Company's carpenter was commissioned to provide a defence to stop unruly passers-by from relieving themselves against the front door of Cutlers' Hall. Nothing changes much, does it?

In 1634, at a banquet, one liveryman threw a bowl of wine at another liveryman called Jasper Churchill who threw two bowls back at him. Tom Girtin's history of the Company reveals that Beadles in particular could be pretty boisterous. He tells us: "Beadles often behaved in an indecent and rude manner and left the Company's account books in taverns." Well, we're a lot better behaved these days. I'm sure that the present Master would not be tempted to try on what the Master Miles Banks tried on in 1617: "He fraudulently got himself elected as Renter Warden too. He was ordered by the Court to give up the post and, when he refused, he was committed to Newgate prison."

And what macabre entertainments were enjoyed. One year, a cook was boiled in a cauldron at Smithfield, for he had tried to poison the Bishop of Rochester. On another occasion, a great tournament was being held in Cheapside in the presence of Edward III and his Queen, the French Ambassador, the Mayor and the Sheriffs... and the scaffolding on which the ladies were standing collapsed. It is an indication of the dyspeptic temper common to those times that the life of the carpenter was in grave danger until the Queen went on her knees to her lord and begged his clemency.

Girtin tells us: "There was the ancient ceremony of the presentation of a deer to the Dean of St Paul's, and this was carried into the cathedral and met by the Dean and Chapter wearing vestments with designs of deer on them... and the deer's head carried round the cathedral on a pole... and a mass said...and everyone given a dinner...

"And fighting in the street between the Fishmongers' Company and the Skinners' Company...between the Goldsmiths' and the Merchant Taylors'... the ringleaders arrested by the Lord Mayor and hanged at Tyburn. ...

"And so many foreigners in London in the reign of Queen Elizabeth I that there were phrasebooks issued in French, Spanish, Italian and

Portuguese. And if you think racism and xenophobia are recent inventions, consider this: in 1550, the Lord Mayor issued a warrant that "no man do or suffer their family or servants in any way to mock, scoff or give any occasion of dissention to any Frenchman or stranger. I'm glad to say he also commanded that no person do mock or scorn any Rectors passing by in the streets, nor throw at them crabs or other unlawful things."

There was another memorable banquet at Cutlers' Hall. It was last Maytime. The interminably wet metropolitan spring seemed finally to be coming to an end. There was a new light over Cheapside, Threadneedle Street and the Embankment. The domes of St Paul's and the Old Bailey gleamed white and gold in the drowsy afternoons. White blouses and short skirts had replaced the funereal overcoats. City gents resenting their neckties. Seventy-two degrees last Sunday, and a warm wind blowing up from the tube stations: dust and a strong hint of the humidity to come. It was the season of Election Services, when in all the great livery companies last year's Master becomes Past Master and a new Master is proclaimed. These ancient and solemn rites take place in the inexpressible splendour of white and gold of our Wren churches – and of course, as they should be, these occasions are followed by some fine banquets. It is in this season that I warm most strongly to Dr Johnson's declaration: "The man who is tired of London is tired of life".

Old London, traditional London – and as I write a full peel is ringing behind me from the twelve bells of Old Bailey – is the City and its timeless institutions. Smithfield Market, a hundred yards from my front door, where we buy all our beef, pork and lamb. And homemade sausages unsurpassable. Last time I went to the Market I was in my shorts. The cheekiest of my five butchers – imagine an elf with a cleaver and a manic grin – said, "'Ere, Vicar, you've got two pieces of cotton hanging down from your waistband!"

I fell for it and looked.

"Oh sorry, guv, my mistake: I see now, them's your legs!"

He sees ghosts, this butcher, and I shall have more to say about him later.

Smithfield Market. Then the Bangladeshi Cockneys of Brick Lane and the little cafes where you can get the best curries this side of

Madras. Spitalfields and St Mary-le-Bow. The easy-going cosmopolitan summer, and no one gives a damn what colour you are and what your accent sounds like: a vast, friendly neighbourliness where no one hates blacks, browns, sky-blue pinks, or even whites; but where people of all shades and hues hate the burglars, the muggers and the Bank Holiday anarchists of whatever colour.

Speaking of anarchists, last May I was standing at the high altar in St Michael's, celebrating the Friday lunchtime Mass for the City workers, when I heard background noise which sounded as if the wind was getting up. Within a few minutes, it roared like a tsunami. I could hardly hear my own voice, so I guess the little congregation could hear nothing at all. I finished the service and went out, still in my vestments, and stood at the top of the church steps as the slouching horde with painted faces lumbered by, snarling their politics of envy. One of them stuck his chin right under my nose and asked, "What are you doing for anti-capitalism, creep?"

I said, "I'm Chaplain to the Stock Exchange." I raised my right hand and started to recite the Exorcism Service in Latin.

The reality was not funny. I fought my way through the mob to get home. The police hadn't expected a disturbance on that scale and they had a terrible job trying, vastly outnumbered as they were, to preserve order. Later that evening, when things had calmed down, I walked down to church with my wife to see if any damage had been done to St Michael's. Luckily, not. But the whole area of the City around the Bank of England, the Stock Exchange and the Royal Exchange (my parish) was a waste-land. The pavements and roads were littered with glass from smashed windows. There was a trail of filth everywhere. Strange, isn't it, how the preferred litter dropped by the anti-globalisation freaks consists of fast-food wrappers and cans of Coca Cola? Strange, too, that anti-capitalists should choose to co-ordinate their vicious excesses with the aid of that supreme emblem of the City yuppie – the mobile phone. Strangest of all, that people who claim to be political idealists should behave like savages.

Later that evening, I learnt that the offices of the LIFFE building had been stormed by the axe-bearing mob. They actually managed to penetrate the first line of defence and broke into the reception area. For a long time, business offices, embassies and other public buildings, anticipating outbreaks of savagery, did not locate their offices on the ground floor, but, as it were, went up higher. A good job, too, that particular teatime at the LIFFE. The murderous thugs tried to run up the elevators and break in to where the financial executives were at their desks and assault them. But they did not bargain for the entrepreneurial nous of the security officers who, by pressing a button at the precise moment, reversed the elevators and turned the barbarians back down upon themselves in a heap.

That was potentially the most serious incursion of the day. If the security guards had not kept their presence of mind, I'm sure there would have been fatalities. There nearly was a murder when, outside the Bank of England, the mob managed to manhandle a policewoman from her horse. Luckily – providentially? – again there were other officers on hand and the mob was beaten back. Any sympathy one might be inclined to have for the political opinions of the anti-capitalists evaporates when one observes at close hand the full, howling hatred of their modus operandi.

Anyhow, the City has seen off worse than that filthy lot before now. And the business of Election Services and banquets was not interrupted. I went to that great banquet at Cutlers' Hall. I sat next to a venerable member who looked, dressed and spoke like a character out of Dickens. Under those elegant chandeliers and emboldened by some magnificent Company claret – the Company gives me a case every Christmas: let that please the anarchists – he told me how, as a septuagenarian, he had just been for his (as he called it) "MOT medical". They had taken his pulse and his blood-pressure, tested him to near-destruction on an exercise machine and then sat him down to ask some personal questions. Although, in the telling of his story, this admirable gentleman certainly erred on the side of restraint, as I listened, I could hardly swallow my roast pork for hysterics:

"Well, the doctor asked me if I had butter on my bread. I said, 'Of course I have butter on my bread! What do you have on yours – blancmange?' Then he got on to eggs: 'How many eggs do you have a week?' I told him straight: 'I always have two for breakfast with my bacon and fried bread. Then we have salad on Saturday and Sunday for tea, and the wife usually chops in half a dozen hard-boiled. And then there there's cakes and pies... Put me down for thirty.'

71

"You should have seen the look on his face. He stared at me as if I should be dead. I told him I've always eaten eggs like that – and taken my steak with a nice bit of fat on, and bacon, pork pies, plenty of chips, bread with butter spread thick so you can taste it. And my wife's butterfly buns with cream, and steamed puddings with treacle.

" 'How many units of alcohol do you consume in a week?' I told him I didn't know what he was talking about – units? I said I'd always enjoyed a drink in moderation: a couple of G&Ts before lunch; the same before dinner (or whisky macs if the weather was cold); a bottle of wine with the meal and a few glasses of port after; a single malt before bed...

"When he'd finished all his silly questions, I said, 'What's the verdict then, doc? How is my blood pressure?'

"'A little on the low side, actually.'"

When I say that the ancient liveries have long been creative contributors to the developed richness of the English language, that is not quite what I had in mind. I meant to refer to such time-laden phrases as "sixes and sevens", which dates from the Middle Ages when there was a dispute between the Skinners and the Merchant Taylors about the order of precedence of company barges following the Lord Mayor up the Thames: who should be sixth in line and who seventh? In the end, a judgement was made to rival the wisdom of Solomon and it was declared that the companies should alternate annually between being sixth in order of precedence and seventh.

I mentioned the Master Mariners as one of the "hands-on" companies – every member of the livery is a sometime Master Mariner. There is a maritime picturesqueness about the Honourable Company's headquarters, which is the good ship HQS Wellington, anchored at Temple Stairs along the Victoria Embankment. It was a naval vessel, converted in 1947 to be the home of the Mariners who were founded in 1926 and given unusual title of "Honourable" by King George V. The lovely teak staircase, which leads down into what is now the main dining-room, was salvaged from the break-up of the Irish "packet" Viper at the time of the conversion. There is a well-stocked library and a model room, full of ships' bells and medals.

Talk about the English tradition in painting being brought to life. One day in May I presided at the marriage of the Clerk to Company's daughter and, after a suitably swashbuckling service at St Michael's, we went back to the HQS Wellington for the reception. In the open air on the top deck in a misty evening light, the sun like a cricket ball falling behind three distant chimneys, the Thames dappled, multi-coloured. It was exactly like a painting by Turner.

The Mariners do a nice line in curry lunches, and you experience the novelty of the dining-room moving with the ebb and flow of the tide. You get the chance to ask questions of the old sea dogs – about, for instance, how to stop a 100,000-ton oil tanker in the shortest distance. One gnarled, whiskered old Mariner gestured with his skinny hand over his chicken Madras and said, "You steer in a circle. Simple, really." But there is nothing simple about the Mariners.

I remember at one of the curry lunches telling the Mariners about a nightmarish crossing from the Isle of Man to Morecambe Bay, and another time when my wife and I were nearly drowned off the north Devon coast. I remember these times because for me they were strange and unusual. But a retired Captain said, "A mariner will forget the number of times he came close to drowning and still love the sea. As Ferdinand says, 'Though the seas threaten, they are merciful.' For the mariner, the sea is his element. What do they know of the world who only know the land? The sea is more than three-fifths of the whole surface of the globe. All life began in the sea, and no one has adequately explained why we ever bothered to crawl out of it!"

This Captain, this Mariner, reminded me rather of the Ancient Mariner. I made friends with him and I was often invited to his house in Chislehurst. He turned out to be a deep reader in the poetry of the ocean, and he would speak of the wine-dark sea and Odysseus tied to the mast to hear the sirens' song while his men rowed on, their ears plugged against the seductive sound of the sea witches. One day when I, a mere landlubber, said, "I have to preach at the Master Mariners' Annual Service. What can I say?" he immediately replied:

"Read them some poetry." He took down an anthology and read me the opening part of Ezra Pound's Canto I:

> And then went down to the ship,
> Set keel to breakers, forth on the godly sea, and
> We set up mast and sail on that swart ship,

Bore sheep aboard her, and our bodies also
Heavy with weeping, and winds from sternward
Bore us out onward with bellying canvas,
Circe's this craft, the trim-coiffed goddess.
All in a hot and copper sky
The bloody sun at noon,
Right up above the mast did stand
No bigger than the moon.

I took his advice and read it. There was a palpable silence through-out the church. Ezra Pound – he's supposed to be for "elitists", isn't he?
The way they received his verse just shows again that preachers don't, mustn't, talk down to their congregations. Hidden depths, so to speak.
I turned the whole sermon into a poetry reading and followed up the Pound with those famous lines by Matthew Arnold from his The Sea of Faith:

Come to the window, sweet is the night air!

Only, from the long line of spray
Where the sea meets the moon-blanched land,
Listen! you hear the grating roar
Of pebbles which the waves draw back and fling,
At their return, up the high strand,
Begin, and cease, and then again begin,
With tremulous cadence slow...

Can You Open a Bank Account in the City of London?

Have you ever tried to open a bank account in the City of London? We at St Michael's haven't been able to manage it – and we've been here longer than the banks. Here we are, a church founded in 179 AD on the site of the ancient Roman forum, adjacent to the Bank of England, the Royal Exchange, the Stock Exchange and Mansion House. When I first came here I saw it as one of my first tasks to set up a Trust Fund to guarantee the finances of our excellent choir. Now, dear reader, as they say, read on preserving, if you will, that degree of imagination which is the temporary suspension of disbelief.

Our church already has an account with the Royal Bank of Scotland, and so for the sake of convenience I decided to open the music account with their branch in Cheapside. I acquired the necessary forms and the three other Trustees and I filled them in. My fellow Trustees are all Christian gentlemen, professional men of good reputation in the City. The bank's application forms reminded me of the sort of tedious, overblown, paranoid documents which Joseph K. was repeatedly asked to fill out in Kafka's The Trial. But, I thought, it's all in a good cause, and I gritted my teeth and steeled myself to the alien bureaucracy – taking with me names, addresses, one set of identification to prove our identities and another to prove our addresses. We completed the tautologically inane section which asked us to declare the purpose of the Music Trust: to provide for the church's music, would you believe? (As in: the object of fishing? Fish.) Well, there are believers and there are sceptics – and then there are banks.

Bearing this sheaf of rigmarole, I turned up at the bank. The cashier leapt forward all obliging smiles and "How can I help yew?" I told her I would like to open a bank account. The look which spread across her face could not have been more startled if I had reached for a sawn-off shotgun and said, "Stick 'em up!"

"But you can't open an account just like that, Sir."

"I have all the necessary documentation and several hundred pounds to pay in straight away. And it's not as if it's an account on which we want to borrow any money – just to service the cheques in and out for our Music Trust."

She looked at me as if I was plumb dumb. To encourage her – I almost said to facilitate her, but that might sound risqué coming from a conservative clergyman – I presented my two sets of identification and told her that our church had an account with them already. She gave me the custom's officer stare and went away to take a photocopy of my passport and confirmation of address. Turning, Medusa-like, she asked if I had included my telephone number on the application form.

"Oh yes, I think so. There's everything else there: date of birth, eye colour, grandmother's wedding day…"

I must say she was tolerant of my mild facetiousness and she said, "The manager will phone you today or tomorrow and arrange an appointment when you can come in and discuss your requirements."

"But I'm here now, and I've told you what I would like!"

"We don't do things like that, Sir."

"You mean, if someone comes into your bank and wants to do some straightforward business, you say this is, of course, possible; but it will have to be done on another day? What's wrong with today, at this moment in time, now?"

"I'm sorry, Sir: it's security."

"What's security? You know us. We're 'valued customers', as your advertising section keeps telling us in your plethora of junk mail."

She merely shook her head and I was left to reflect on the astonishing phenomenon of a bank's refusing to take my hard cash. The manager did not phone that day, or the next, or the day after that. So, on the following Monday, I phoned the bank. By chance the manager herself answered the telephone and I reported the whole misadventure. She was extremely nice and conciliatory, saying, "I'm afraid you were given some wrong information: you don't have to have an appointment with me in order to open an account."

I was seized by a rush of euphoria, such as one might feel upon having been told that one was not, after all, going to be hanged the next morning. I was reassured that the bank would inaugurate the account "…as soon as I identify the person who has your paperwork on their desk."

Next day, another cashier phoned to tell me I must make an appointment to open the account. It was like going round and round in a revolving door. I said. "But I've spoken to the manager about this."

The cashier then put the manager herself on the phone. She explained, "When you said that your church already banks with us – and I have checked this, of course..." [she spoke fiercely, as one instinctively suspicious of all Christian institutions] "...I thought the matter would be simple. But it isn't, because the names of the signatories to your Music Trust are different from the names that appear on your normal account."

"Of course they are! I don't expect the same four people to do all the work that the church needs to do! But please tell me, how can I proceed as quickly as possible to get this account opened?"

Then she began to rehearse the protocols of the gulag: "We shall need two sets of identification..."

"I've already given you three."

"...but for each signatory. Their passports and driving licences. And six months' bank statements for each."

The idiom was infectious. I said, "Will you put that in writing – in triplicate – so that I and my colleagues know exactly what is required of us – then I shan't be wasting any more of your time?"

"I'm sorry, Sir, but to engage in such correspondence is no part of the bank's policy. I will, though, contact you officially at a later date."

Each morning, I am up early lying in wait for Postman Pat, and trying to reassure myself that the City of London really is the most efficient financial centre in the world.

Over My Dead Body

These days I am not obliged to keep a constant lookout in case medical students from St Bartholomew's Hospital try to steal corpses from my graveyard. My home is called "the Watch House" because, in the 19th century, my predecessors, the former Rectors of St Sepulchre-without-Newgate, were paid an extra £30 per annum to inform on the grave-robbers. These rogues – or progressive humanitarians, according to your will - used to dig up the corpses from our churchyard and take them across the road to the basement of the local pub where they would be labelled – a little note around the cold toe – for this or that surgeon: £10 a body.

Actually, the Victorians were not as prudish – quite – as they are sometimes made out to be. The 19th century authorities did allow a number of male bodies to be used for anatomical demonstrations, but they thought it unseemly to allow female bodies. This is the epitome of Victorian sentimentality and it reminds me of Thomas Huxley's words at a meeting of the Royal Association to Bishop Samuel Wilberforce at the time of the Darwinian controversy: "If the Right Reverend gentleman is willing to allow his ancestry on his grandfather's side to be traced to that of a monkey, would he be so willing to have it thus traced on his grandmother's side?"

Our area of the City was the centre of the vice trade for five hundred years – not for nothing is the nearest street to the north of the church named Cock Lane. So there were plenty of prostitutes buried in our churchyard, and it was their corpses which were so much in demand by the experimental surgeons.

St Sepulchre's church has such a benign atmosphere that I would not hesitate to spend the night on the chancel floor. Indeed, one of my friends from Yorkshire insists on doing just that whenever he visits us. Strange that the atmosphere should be so benign when you think of some of our church's historical connections. The Old Bailey, just across the road, now stands on the site of the infamous Newgate Prison. My predecessors played a grisly role in connection with this old jail and I have the relic in church to remind me of it. This is the execution bell with which the Parish Clerk used to summon the condemned man to repentance the night before he was due to be hanged. He would walk down through a subterranean passageway and ring the bell outside the condemned cell.

This macabre bell is mentioned in Macbeth: "It was the owl that shrieked which gave the fatal bellman his stern'st goodnight." Shakespeare used to pass along Newgate Street on his way to the Globe theatre and he would have heard the execution bell on many occasions. Two other old phrases are associated with the executions of prisoners held in Newgate: "In the cart" – meaning in trouble – derives from the practice of taking the condemned to be hanged at Tyburn in a cart. The other familiar expression is "going west" – meaning to be on the way out – for of course Tyburn was to the west of the City. Custom shows that, if the condemned was well-liked among the local populace, he would be plied with many drinks "in the cart" on the way to his execution. If he was not liked, he would be pelted with rotten fruit. In our church tower we still house the twelve bells of Old Bailey, mentioned in the nursery rhyme, Oranges and Lemons.

On the front wall of the Watch House, built in 1791, we have a treasure: the carved stone bust of Charles Lamb (1775-1834), famous for his joint authorship, with his sister Mary, of the Tales from Shakespeare. Lamb had been at Christ's Hospital School, just around the corner, where his best friend was the great poet and critic Samuel Taylor Coleridge. Lamb's life-story makes for tragic reading. A gifted writer, a genial man with enormous wit and profound human sympathies – who else could have described the deeply troubled Coleridge as "an archangel, a little damaged"? – he seemed to have a successful literary career lined up before him when, in 1796, his sister went mad and stabbed their invalid mother to death. Just twenty-one years old, Charles promised the magistrates that he would be guardian to Mary for the rest of her life – thus saving her from permanent imprisonment.

It is ironic that in the Tales from Shakespeare Mary wrote the comedies and Charles the tragedies! Worn out by his responsibilities, Charles died in 1834 and Mary lived on for a further thirteen years.

So much for the front of the Watch House. What lies at the rear is even more spectacular. If I go through our kitchen door and turn left, I am immediately in the chancel of the ancient church of St Sepulchre itself, the largest church in the City of London and named after the Holy Sepulchre in Jerusalem. The second Crusade was launched from here in AD 1104.

Walk westwards out of the chancel, down the blue-carpeted nave and turn towards the south aisle. Here is a stained glass window commemorating John Smith, the adventurer, who set off from this parish in his three little ships in 1607 and founded the Commonwealth of Virginia. The story is well-known: how he was captured by Indians and rescued by Pocahontas whom he brought back to England, and she died at Gravesend. This piece of history features in Disney's film Pocahontas where, alas, the facts are not allowed to get in the way of a Hollywood melodrama.

We had a melodrama of our own. One October Sunday, the crime fiction writer Patricia Cornwell – of the forensic inclination and cadaverous imagination – turned up at the Watch House with her coterie and asked to be shown the church interior. This lady is given to sudden lavish acts of generosity: only the week before, she had left a £10,000 tip following luncheon at a country pub – just because she had appreciated the quality of service. We were instantly treated to a dose of the same largesse as she gazed at the John Smith window and declared, "I'd like to pay for another window here in honour of Pocahontas."

Well, we set the procedures in motion. It so happened that, the following spring, the Governor of Virginia was scheduled to pay a visit to England. This was in my year as Chaplain to the Lord Mayor. I managed to arrange a reception in church one bright May morning, graced by both the Lord Mayor and the Governor – and kindly paid for by the Governor himself. We invited journalists from The Times and The Telegraph and documentary-makers from several TV channels. The sun blazed through the John Smith window, and through the clear panes in the window adjacent which Ms Cornwell had so graciously offered to decorate. There were short, cheerful speeches of transatlantic cordiality and then Ms Cornwell seized the rostrum. Out of the blue she announced – her outstretched arm indicating every point of the compass - that she did not want to put in a single window to Pocahontas, but seven windows illustrating the historic link between our church and the Commonwealth of Virginia.

Naturally, we ran into trouble. First, there was no chance that the diocesan authorities or the bureaucrats in English Heritage would ever allow seven windows to be installed commemorating our connections with Virginia: for to do this would make our ancient church seem like a mere satellite of that US State. Secondly, the Indians objected: it was thought to be racist and patronising that we should conjecture installing an image of the young woman who rescued John Smith. As things stand, we are negotiating a single window to mark our happy connections with Virginia – a single window that will both escape the censure of the arty-farty types in English Heritage and steer wide of the Native Americans' accusations of political incorrectness.

On the opposite side of the church – on the north aisle – is the world famous Musicians' Chapel where the ashes of Sir Henry Wood, Founder of the Promenade Concerts in 1895 – are interred. Henry learnt the organ at St Sepulchre's as a boy and there are delicious stories of how his tutor would give the boy his lesson and then leave for The Viaduct pub across the road while Henry practised. Young Henry, being a precocious little chap, would soon perfect his lesson and go over the road to the pub to ask his tutor what he ought to do next. These stories would indicate in the most delicate terms that his master told him exactly what he should do. The Viaduct pub still stands, and I have got into the habit of disappearing into it quite a bit myself.

Of course he was a populariser, but he never dumbed down. As well as what Beecham called "lollipops" at the Proms, Wood played original works by controversial living composers. Mahler, Stravinsky's Firebird and the Five Orchestral Pieces by Arnold Schoenberg. And in 1898 he played Wagner's Parsifal at a concert attended by Queen Victoria who asked him, "Are you quite English?" He got drunk with Max Reger, and once advised Gustav Holst to go to Margate for a rest cure. Because of his practice of performing familiar music alongside what was new, he drew from the rugged and radical Ethyl Smyth the compliment, "God bless Henry for introducing mixed bathing in music!" There is a nice story concerning Henry and Ethyl. Wood recalls: "A man came to repair my bicycle. I saw him leaning over the piano and looking out of the window. He had his back to me and I noticed his wide breeches which were not unlike plus fours. I called out, 'Thank you for coming so promptly. I want you to look at my bicycle.'

"The figure at the piano turned round and spoke: 'Bicycle? I am no bicycle. I am Ethyl Smyth!'"

"The lot hath fallen unto me in a fair ground," as the Psalmist says. There is nowhere in the world lovelier than the Church of the Holy Sepulchre. When the sun pours through the south window and seems to light the altar candles, incandescent, from the inside of them, all the tender associations of the faith flood the mind and senses: the green hill far away without the City wall – just as we are – and the cave in the rock, the place where they laid him. I would wish for nothing more – except perhaps to escape the fate of one of my illustrious predecessors, John Rogers, Rector of this parish and assistant to William Tyndale, translator of the Bible into English, who was the first Protestant martyr, burnt at the stake for his pains in 1555, where now I buy the Sunday joint, on Smithfield Market by Bloody Mary.

New Age Yuppies Steal the Font

I have made strong criticisms of the Church's new worship books on many occasions, but I suppose one should be thankful to find a church using a worship book of any sort rather than the lurid example of a service I came across at a City christening. A family of New Age bankers – no, I'm not making this up – had gathered to giggle round the font. Here was a brisk experience of culture shock. As I entered the medieval church the huge congregation was singing and clapping to the words:

> Spirit of the living God, fall afresh on me;
> Break me, melt me, mould me, fill me....

The choir came in almost at a gallop and obviously preferred talking and laughing among themselves to singing the silly words to the babyish tune. Then here comes the Vicar, smile on full beam, vigorously joining in the clapping. It was not so much a procession as an outbreak of the conga. As he swung into the central aisle, I got a close view of his vestments which looked as if they had been designed by Walt Disney: cherubs with grins as wide as the Vicar's against a symbol like a pop logo. The back of his chasuble was, I was told later, supposed to portray the Holy Spirit descending to earth, but it was more like Monty Python's dead parrot falling off its perch.

When he got to the chancel step, he spun round and the banana-split smile stretched wider still and wider. He raised his hands high and the gaudy chasuble opened so that he resembled a huge, technicoloured moth. He bawled a stentorian greeting" "Hello!" It was the way he said it: a very long "hell" and a very short "O". The congregation bawled back "Hello!" with the same intonation. Then he yelled, "Nice to see you!" and cocked his hand behind his ear inviting the people to yell back, "To see you, nice!" – just like they do on the Saturday evening television game shows. There was no opening prayer, as such. Instead, the Vicar started to chat: "We are here for a very special event. This is going to be an exciting day for Clive and Tracey [the said bankers] and a very special day too for little Sidonie Clarissa." Then he intoned a long sentimental, "Ahh!" and the congregation echoed in chorus.

I noticed the family sitting in the front pew: Clive in suede shoes and a white suit matching Sidonie's shawl; Tracey in a dress that could only be described as a gownless evening strap. The Vicar continued in his Noddy language: "After our special prayer, Sidonie Clarissa will be welcomed as a full member of our church family." And he added, "How about that then?" – just like Jimmy Savile used to do on Jim'll Fix It. The congregation howled with laughter at this profound witticism. Belatedly, I realised that the christening was going to be included within the service of Holy Communion. "But first..." he intoned, just like the BBC announcer "...we'll all join in singing another of my favourite songs." He bellowed the whole of the first verse as an example, in case the intellectual content of the words should prove too taxing for his congregation:

> Sing Alleluia to the Lord,
> Sing Alleluia to the Lord
> Sing Alleluia, sing Alleluia
> Sing Alleluia to the Lord.

I'm not making this up either: this "song" can be found, number S.22 in Hymns for Today's Church. That hymn book only convinces us that "today's" Church is a lot more dumbed-down than yesterday's. We stopped to get our breath back and the running commentary resumed: "Now we are going to tell God how sorry we are for all the things we have done wrong..." I felt like saying, "Let's begin with a suitably grovelling apology for the goings-on here this morning."

The Vicar chortled, "We turn to the prayer of confession on page 36 of the green booklet..." A great rustling of paper among the penitents. He went on, "Now let us stand and express our faith in the words of the Creed. Turn to page 43. Today we are using the seventh alternative prayer of consecration to be found on page 96 and the optional thanksgiving, second part, on page 123..." I'd heard of painting by numbers: this was religion by numbers.

But first, as he said, we were here to witness Sidonie Clarissa's christening. He asked us to sit down while the modern parents made their way to the font, grinning at their fellow hippy-yuppies as they went, and the hippy-yuppies grinning back. It was then that I first noticed a piece of paper on my seat. Everybody had one: grey and heavy, like pretend parchment with writing on in a script like the Indian rope trick. The Vicar stood beaming luminously by the font and began to read from the grey paper: "Introducing the godparents; Emma and Steven…" There was a round of applause as the two of them stood up. Step forward then the gorgeous couple: Emma in a kaftan and Steven bearded and wearing flip flops and a single earring the size of the Koh-i-Noor. Each had a smile to rival the Vicar's.

"Let me tell you a few things about this lovely couple who are to be Sidonie Clarissa's sponsors today. Emma is a producer with an independent television company making films on social issues for Channel Four. She and Steven took the courageous decision to travel the world with their own three children, staying in spiritual ashrams before returning to England to live for a year in a special religious centre devoted to the idea that belief in God and atheism amount to the same thing. Steven, of course, is a top journalist involved in the production of technical texts and computer programmes for a management training company. They are both greatly committed to the counselling process, having trained at the Guild of Pastoral Psychology. I know that Clive and Tracey will be glad to know that Emma and Steven have a very empowering and positive attitude towards parenting. They have asked me to thank you all for sharing with them today and hope that we will all in this service play a positive role in the life of Sidonie Clarissa. So let's hear it for Emma and Steven…"

More applause. Then, taking the baby in his arms and drooling his perpetual effulgence over her, he prayed, "In the name of the Lord Krishna, Shiva, the great Buddha – and of Jesus, whom some call Lord – and of all prophets and masters everywhere who have taught peace and enlightenment, we welcome Sidonie Clarissa into the family where true relationships are celebrated." He poured water over the infant from a sea shell, lifted her to his smiling chops and kissed her with a deliberate loudness which caused the congregation to laugh – but made the baby cry.

Next, the giant, luminous, ecclesiastical moth outspread his arms and drifted back towards the sanctuary where he shouted at us: " Let us offer one another a sign of peace!"

Whereupon all hell broke loose. People strolled or ran about the place at will, seizing and hugging one another, kissing and cuddling, exchanging, here and there, little pieces of gossip about who had been at last night's disco; some laughing, but others weeping at the sheer emotional depth of it all, I suppose. A large lady in a kilt set eyes on me from afar. She trundled up the aisle and smothered me in her cardigan. Though the woolly sleeves covered my ears, I still heard her shriek her message of peace. I doubt if she heard my whispered response to her overtures: "No thank you madam – I'm English!"

There was another "song" of the Let's Jog for Jesus sort. Then, seen off by the Vicar, his ethereal handshake and over-friendly smile, we walked the three hundred yards to the great livery hall where the spiritually much-travelled parents and godparents – if they will forgive me for bringing God into a baptism – set before us food and wine and speeches which the libel laws compel me to leave unreported.

The Automatic Ecclesiastical Switchboard

The parish clergy are constantly deluged with communications from the central church authorities – you might call it ecclesiastical junk mail. The other week I was invited on a course "to improve your communication skills". This was to be run – believe it or not – by the "Diocesan Communications Officer". You would think they were operating a Central Department for Tautology. There are similar courses on youth work, fundraising and church music. Of course, when they say "church music", they don't mean Tallis, Byrd, Palestrina and Bach: they mean the jogging for Jesus choruses which you read out, as you clap, from the screen at the front – just as if you were at a pantomime. If you visit churches which do that sort of thing, you soon discover that you are at a pantomime.

Most of the ecclesiastical junk mail that falls through the letterbox is generally inane and usually badly written, the pages of details ornamented by little cartoon figures – perhaps sucking a pencil with a "thinks" bubble over his head. What am I saying, "his"? Political correctness has taken over in the Church as it has done everywhere else, so there is now always among these infantile drawings a careful mix of women and men, blacks, whites and browns, old and infirm, disabled and so on.

What's more, it's a strange thing that, while the diocese confesses that it no longer has any money to support the priests, it still contrives to employ all these "advisers" and "officers". The Communications Officer we have met already: then there is the Education Adviser, who is a different person from the Children's Officer. Add to these the Mission Adviser, quite distinct from the Adviser for Evangelism, the Training Officer, the Urban Ministry Adviser and half a dozen others while noting there is a shortage of parish priests, and you are reminded of the startling bureaucratic comparison with the once great Royal Navy which now boasts more admirals than ships.

As an example of this ecclesiastical junk mail, I can't do better than tell you about the Church's policies for the care of children. Along with every other clergyman in the Diocese of London, I received a forty-page glossy booklet called Children: Promoting Their Welfare, Protecting Them From Harm. It reads like jargon from the Circumlocution Office, peppered with bullet points and full of the same mixture of sentimentality and bullying we find in the MacPherson Report. At a time when the Diocese is pleading poverty and raising the amount the parishes have to pay each year to central funds, it is surprising to see them lashing out on expensive publications of this sort. But the content of the booklet makes me despair for the mind of the Church.

It begins with portentous statements of the obvious: "Children need love, affection and encouragement; physical care and nurture; protection from physical dangers; security and control which is firm, clear consistent and kind." The next sentence also looks as if it was generated by that famous Ecclesiastical Department for Tautology: "Physical abuse may involve hitting, shaking, throwing, poisoning, burning or scalding, drowning, suffocating or otherwise causing physical harm to a child." I have yet to discover that our organist is a serial poisoner or that the parish clerk is just bursting to drown a Confirmation candidate.

But where the document is not pleonastic and banal, it is meaningless. It goes on to say, "Those working with children and young people should be carefully selected." But by whom? As I understand it, the problem of child abuse in the Church takes the form of abuse by parsons and other Church officers – the very people who are here being invited to select new colleagues. It's the old question: Who will guard the guardians? Unabashed, it continues, "Team members should monitor one another in the area of physical contact." Apart from the fact that this injunction is sure to create group paranoia and institutionalise distrust, the obvious truth is that anyone who wants to abuse a child will do so when there is no one else watching.

It says that those who work with children should be "trained". Trained in what? Presumably Sunday School teachers can teach and choirmasters can impart musical understanding. The idea there is something additional to their skills in which they must be "trained" is merely a superstitious fad believed like an article of faith by educationists and social workers. It says, "Each parish is required to appoint a Children's Advocate who could be introduced and interviewed during the main Sunday Service." What, and ruin another act of Divine Worship?

And then, "Choirmasters, organists, bell-ringers and others who are likely to give individual tuition should follow their professional code of ethics." Well, what else? They'll be suggesting we should pay our taxes and not be unkind to small animals next. But, "Private tuition should not be given on church premises without another adult being present." It isn't always possible for another adult to be present, but in any case two adults can inflict twice as much abuse as one: Mr and Mrs West made an efficient team, didn't they?

Under the heading "Confidentiality", it says, "Having a relationship with a grown up who listens, encourages and affirms can be hugely valuable to a child." (What would the denial of that statement amount to? But never mind). "Such a relationship will allow for 'good' secrets." How is it that the self-appointed experts, the Diocesan Children's Adviser and the four "Child Protection Advisers", who have produced this ridiculous manual don't understand that perverts know exactly – better than the advisers – how to listen, encourage and affirm and otherwise manipulate a child's confidence? In the sickening jargon of child abuse, the process is known as "grooming".

Incredibly, the manual assures us, "Children should know that adults may be trusted not to betray confidences." Which adults? The statement merely begs the question which the manual sets out to answer – that of how to prevent child abuse by identification of the abusers. And, "Gossip and rumour-mongering are to be discouraged as inconsistent with the Christian life, but whistle-blowing is not." Unless the authors are first to abolish Original Sin, how are we to tell the difference? All this "monitoring" and "whistle-blowing" reminds us of the Soviet system under Stalin.

The inanity of it all is stultifying: "Don't touch inappropriately or intrusively." Anyone who is not an abuser knows this without benefit of a bureaucratic, governessy lecture. "Don't give lifts to children or young people on their own. If this is unavoidable, ask the child to sit in the back." But this sort of unfriendly, antisocial behaviour is itself a form of abuse. Besides, if I saw a child standing alone in the churchyard in the rain and called out "Quick, get in the back of the car!" the poor mite would think he was being kidnapped.

I was thinking of a way to respond to this rubbish: "Every year at the Annual Vestry Meeting, each Church Council shall appoint a parish paedophile. He/she must not abuse only little white boys but must observe good practice and equal opportunities. Sexism and racism are strictly forbidden: white and black, male and female, whatever their gender, children should all receive an equal share of abuse..."

But no, when the Church is as far gone into the realms of idiocy and waste as to produce Children: Promoting Their Welfare, satire becomes impossible.

I've been on some crazy diocesan courses in my time, but nowadays I tend to stay away. Occasionally, I feel a pang of guilt, feeling that I'm not joining in and being sociable. But when you relent and turn up, it's always the same: the musty smell of the church hall; the plastic cup of this brown stuff which they dole out at "Coffee and Welcome"; the chairman's opening speech with its jokes even weaker than the coffee; and then the expert's jargon followed by the hackneyed practice of "splitting into groups". The end comes with the "Plenary Session" in which "group leaders" report to the whole assembly – usually remarks that were never made in the first place. Finally, the chairman comes back and says, "Well, we've heard a most stimulating range of opinions, but the most important part of the day has been the chance to meet and interact..." Out into the street then and the burning consciousness of yet another chronicle of wasted time.

You might think that the glossy booklet about the care of children is just about as silly as anyone could get – but no. Last month the Diocese sent me a leaflet advertising a course. And the purpose of the course was "...to teach the clergy and other parish workers how to say 'No' when they are asked to attend a course". As an exercise in futility, it beats Waiting for Godot.

I once attended a course provided by the Communications Officer to teach us how to write letters, to answer the door and the telephone. We were all asked to supply details in advance of how we did things in our particular parishes. I couldn't resist replying in a form that surely would win approval in today's Church, which strains every sinew to appear "modern":

I have installed a fully automatic switchboard at the Rectory...

Hello, you have reached St Trendy's Rectory. If you have a star button on your telephone, press it TWICE now and listen CAREFULLY to the following FIVE possible options:

If you want Matins or Evensong, press ONE.

For Holy Communion, press TWO.

For hatches, matches and despatches, press THREE.

If you would like to subscribe to our covenanted giving scheme, press FOUR; or indeed any combination of numbers you like in order to receive the Treasurer's immediate and undivided attention. Better still, press NOTHING AT ALL and call round with your cheque book at once.

Experience showed me that even this sophisticated system stood in need of refinement. I got a call on number TWO asking about Holy Communion. By an oversight, I answered it in person and, because there are so many alternative versions of this service these days, I was on the phone all morning. So I installed the following sub-system:

You have reached St Trendy's Church, Holy Communion Department. If you want The Book of Common Prayer, press ONE. If you want The Alternative Service Book, tough luck, because the General Synod has just banned it. If you want the new Common Worship Book - well, do think CAREFULLY about this decision first, as no refunds will be made to dissatisfied customers – press THREE.

The first caller pressed THREE and, after a blast of my specially chosen recorded music, the hymn Trumpet of God Sound High, Till the Hearts of the Heathen Shake, she got through to my sub-sub-system designed to cope with the almost infinite number of variants in the Common Worship Holy Communion:

If you want Order One in traditional language, press FIVE. If you want Order Two in Noddy language, press NINE. Thank you. Now please listen CAREFULLY to the following TEN possibilities: There

91

are EIGHT Eucharistic Prayers. If you want Prayer One, press ONE. If you want Prayer Two, press TWO, and so on... Be CAREFUL to identify in advance which particular prayer you require, as mistakes cannot be rectified by this system or any sub-systems in this ecclesiastical cybersphere.

For example, if you want the prayer in traditional language beginning, "...who in the same night that He was betrayed, took bread..." press SEVEN. But if you want the prayer in the Noddy language which begins, "He had supper with his friends..." press EIGHT, TWICE, and please remember to specify Savoy Grill, Chinese Takeaway or Barbecue in the Garden. Light the blue touch-paper and put the phone DOWN.

If you want the Annex to Order Two, press THREE, NINE TIMES. If you want the Gospel Acclamations for Ordinary Time, press NINE, THREE TIMES – and do your own explaining to the police. Decide whether you want the Lectionary, the Revised Lectionary, the Revised Common Lectionary (plus Collects in Traditional Language), press EIGHT again and have your credit card handy. For the Alternative Form of Confession (Sexual Misdemeanours, Section 99, paragraph 47) put the phone DOWN, come round immediately, knock THREE times and ask for Sister Wendy.

If you want the Third Exhortation from The Book of Common Prayer, dial the emergency services. And may the Lord have mercy on your soul.

Ghosts

It's not a question of whether we have a ghost at St Michael's, but of how many. I was phoned up one morning by the Secretary of Zion College, an old theological library near the City Temple. He said, "I've come across a large photograph of one of your predecessors. Rather a fine portrait it is too. Would you like to come and collect it?" So I went and picked up the picture which was indeed very handsome: the picture of The Rev'd John Henry Joshua Ellison who was Rector of St Michael's in the early part of the 20th century. I fixed it to the wall in the vestry.

The following Sunday at the parish Communion I was standing at the high altar leading the prayers when suddenly there arose the most furious banging and clattering from the south west corner of the nave. I thought at first it must be an unruly child throwing a tantrum. After a few minutes the noise ceased and I thought no more about it. But at the end of the service all the congregation were agog, discussing the cause of the disturbance. Everyone had heard it – you couldn't help hearing such a loud commotion. And there were no small children in church that morning. One man in particular, a very level-headed chap, an engineer, was seriously frightened. He was trembling even as he told me what he had experienced: "It was happening in my pew – as if someone was stamping his feet angrily or kicking the woodwork. The whole pew was shaking for three or four minutes. Right next to me, it was. But there was no one else in the pew but me." Two people in the pew immediately behind him said they felt the same movements. It was then that the Parish Clerk came forward and said, "I think I know what it was all about...

"Some years ago I was laying out the altar cloth one morning for the service. Nothing spooky about the morning: the sun was lighting the woodwork and the choir were rehearsing. Out of the corner of my eye I noticed a clergyman walking slowly but purposefully up the south aisle towards the vestry. I wondered who it might be since we had not booked a visiting preacher that day. Anyhow, I walked out of the sanctuary, round the side of the chamber organ and into the south aisle to meet him. He walked through the door – which I always keep locked, as we've had things stolen during choir practices - and into the vestry. I rubbed my eyes. I thought I was seeing things! But when I opened the vestry door and went inside, there was no one there.

"I asked older members of the congregation if they had any idea who the ghostly parson might be. From my description of a balding man with an oval face and side whiskers, they told me the figure most resembled a Father Ellison who had been Rector twenty years or more ago.

"A few years after this, we were planning to celebrate the centenary of our association with London Electricity and I was asked to try to arrange for a bishop to come and preach at their annual service. By good fortune, I managed to persuade the then Bishop of London, Dr Gerald Ellison, to come. A month before the service was due to take place, I was at the high altar again when I saw the same ghostly figure – walking swiftly this time, as if a little late, towards the vestry. I ran round to intercept him, but he vanished before I had even got as far as the chamber organ at the head of the south aisle.

"Strange that this apparition of Father Ellison should have turned up – if indeed that is who it was – just a few weeks before his son was booked to preach for us. I told the bishop about the visitation and described the ghostly visitor in as much detail as I could recall. The bishop was most shaken by what I told him and he said, 'That's pa all right. I wonder why he should still be here? I'll pray for him.'

"If a prayer for peace and rest was what was required, then it must have worked, for I never saw the apparition again." The Parish Clerk gave me a severe look: "Except you've gone and put his picture up in the vestry, haven't you? I bet that's what stirred the old boy up and made him rattle the pews!"

I remain to be convinced – though I don't think anyone could explain the commotion in the pew that Sunday morning by merely natural causes. It was, in my view, far too loud and continuous for it to have been the wood expanding or contracting with a change in the temperature of the building. But ghosts in broad daylight? It's a bit hard to swallow. I belong to the fairly sceptical school of thought when it comes to supposedly ghostly manifestations. I might even say I share Ebenezer Scrooge's view that you can put down seeing ghosts to trouble with your digestion. As Scrooge said to the ghost of Jacob Marley: "Why, you could be an undigested piece of cheese! There's more of gravy than grave about you!" Well, all I can say is that the whole congregation must have eaten vast cheesy breakfasts that morning to account for so much clatter.

Father Ellison's ghost was not the only spooky visitation at St Michael's. Our organist who has served here for more than twenty years told me that sometimes when he is practising late at night, all alone in the darkness, he hears strange noises. I asked him, "What do you do?"

"I stop playing whatever I'm practising and play some Bach instead. That always quietens things down!"

Tatty Tate

It's art innit? Or is it? I confess to causing a disturbance at the new Tate Modern Gallery – that re-ordered power-station on the south bank of the Thames at the end of the Millennium bridge. That's the bridge that was closed as soon as it opened, because its architect and builders had not allowed for the fact that the large numbers of people walking across it would cause it to sway unacceptably. Now that the bridge is open again, we can all walk across from St Paul's cathedral to Tate Modern in about five minutes – thus establishing a new shortest distance between the sublime and the ridiculous.

What the Tate needs is a visit from the little boy in Hans Christian Andersen's fairy tale who alone had the courage to announce that the king had no clothes on. In the absence of the little boy, I tried to do his job for him. The so-called "art" in Tate Modern consists mainly of "installations" and an installation is a piece of conceptual art: that is, its aesthetic qualities – what aesthetic qualities? – are secondary to the "idea" of it. So, for example, an installationist might conceive of a carpenter's workshop and then construct the same out of polystyrene. There are plenty of examples of this sort in Tate Modern. One of these structures comes complete with a polystyrene Coca Cola can. Interestingly, some connoisseur of modern art on his trip round the gallery had placed a real Coca Cola can next to the pretend one. One doesn't have to be Andrew Lambirth to see that this raises philosophical questions about the whole aesthetics of the piece.

Room after room of pretentious junk. There is, for another instance, something that resembles the mess that the builders have left at the back of our church while they have been working here these last six months. You see members of the great British public gawping with dumbstruck admiration at this rubbish. I was going to say it's an insult to their intelligence, but then I have to think, what intelligence?

Well, this is where I created my little bit of havoc. I ignored the pile of junk and drew an attendant's notice to a fire door. "Look," I said in my loudest clerical voice, "at that magnificent installation of a fire door!"

"Oh no, Sir, " said the attendant, swiftly and politely correcting my great ignorance, "that's not a work of art: it's a real fire door".

But I persisted, "Oh, do come off it! How can you pretend that a piece of construction so beautiful and finely-wrought is not a work of art?" I began to walk up and down the room, drawing other visitors' attention to the fire door as I went: "Look at the exquisite line! The way that the handle is fixed deliberately on to one side instead of the other. Notice the bold elegance of the red lettering FIRE DOOR. Only a genius would have thought to do that lettering in red. Run the palm of your hand over the surface and feel the texture of the metal. Sense, if you will, the sheer fire-doorishness of this fire door! Something so profoundly beautiful as that is surely a worthy modern successor to Raphael's Pieta or the Mona Lisa of Leonardo!"

In the end, the attendant called for his colleague and they had to restrain me. I protested that what they so rudely called my "making a nuisance of myself" was really my own work of art, my own personal statement of true artistic integrity; my very own installation. I had to leave, but not before I'd thoroughly enjoyed my ten minutes of "artistic freedom"; my finger-pointing, nose turned up mockery.

I must say, though, that Tate Modern does offer access to one supreme work of art. I noticed that, from the second floor, there is the most spectacular view across the river to where stands St Paul's in all its magnificence.

Order of Service to Mark the Passing of the ASB:

commonly called The Burial of the Deadly

The Church of England has been blessed through having a wonderful liturgy written when the English language was at its most sublime. This is of course The Book of Common Prayer put together by Archbishop Thomas Cranmer in the 16th century and given its final form at the Restoration in 1662.

In this book are all those wonderful phrases, hallowed by time and use. I shall just mention a few: "With this ring I thee wed" – six words each of one syllable going back to the time of Chaucer; "Ashes to ashes; dust to dust"; "Lighten our darkness we beseech thee O Lord"; "Almighty God, forasmuch as without thee we are not able to please thee"; "Give us grace that we may cast away the works of darkness and put upon us the armour of light"; "The devil and all his works"; "Who of thy tender mercy didst give thy only Son Jesus Christ to suffer death upon the cross for our redemption". Only, as I said, a few phrases out of what Jeremy Taylor described as "a treasure house of rare devotion".

This book was the centre of the Church's daily and weekly public worship for four centuries, until the tin-eared trendies in the ecclesiastical hierarchy, bishops and the like, decided they could do better. And so in the 1960s they brought out a succession of liturgical pamphlets with bureaucratic titles such as "Series One...Two and Three". The language of these pamphlets, and therefore the theology – because, as C.H.Sisson wrote, "Unfortunately, the choice of words determines what is being said" – was abysmal, incoherent, unmemorable and banal. Alas, the various Series were solidified in 1980 into a vast tome called The Alternative Service Book (ASB) which was ruthlessly promoted by the hierarchy at the expense of the parishes – and largely to their disgust – as "the greatest publishing event in four hundred years".

How odd then, that only twenty years later, the same hierarchs actually banned the ASB. So much for the greatest publishing event in nearly half a millennium! In 2000 they replaced it with Common Worship, another book, even bigger and worse – a sort of book of variants in which the clergy are more or less encouraged to make up the service as they go along; to cut and paste from an almost infinite variety of alternatives and options, so that the effect is reminiscent of the Tower of Babel episode where no one understood anything said by anyone else.

I wouldn't touch Common Worship with a pair of sterilised tongs. We use only The Book of Common Prayer in our churches. People seem to know what they like: our congregation has increased tenfold in four years and we have solemnised the marriages of twenty-two couples in that same period – all according to the old wedding service in the 1662 book. So, far from being alienated by the traditional language, all these couples have become regular attenders; and later this year we are to celebrate a Holy Communion for them all, after which the whole lot of us will go out on the town for a slap-up dinner.

I couldn't resist paying some formal acknowledgement to the demise of the ASB. So I invented the following little service and, together with the organist and choir, we gave that awful 1980 book a decent burial according to the rite set out below:

Each parish church, cathedral or college chapel shall gather together all its copies of the ASB and stand them on an heap at some convenient place in the churchyard. Whereupon the people shall go into the church preceded by the President and singing this hymn following:

> O book no help for not long past
> No hope for years to come;
> We always knew you couldn't last,
> You miserable tome.

> They said you were the greatest thing
> Since plastic-wrapped sliced bread;
> But now they've told us we must sing
> Of how you're very dead.

> Your phrases they were dull and flat,
> And doctrines incomplete;
> Your rhythms dragged along so that
> We thought of rotting meat.

99

You always were a sickly child,
But (my word!) weren't you fat?
Alternatives so thick compiled:
"Some say this some say that".

Your baptisms left Satan out,
Your funerals knew no worms;
With lustless weddings there's no doubt
We could not come to terms.

"Visible and invisible"
"Seen and unseen" came to be;
Irreverent and risible,
Rite "A" was a right "B".

So now we bring you to the fire,
Our hearts are glum and glummer;
Though you were awful, dumb and dire,
The new book is yet dumber.

Tune: St Anne

The President (or the Commissar for women bishops, if she be present) shall then read in a loud voice a Statement from the Chairperson of the Liturgical Commission. This Statement is commonly called:

The Prayers of Penitence

President or, as it might be, Commissar: I have not come to praise the ASB but to bury it. In 1980, we said, "Those who seek to know the mind of the Church of England in the last quarter of the 20th century will find it in the ASB."
All: Gosh! Some mind eh?
P or C: We said at the same time that this book was "the biggest publishing event in 400 years".
All: Oh! Not as big as Harry Potter.
P or C: We hoped it would reverse the decline in church attendance.

All: Instead the congregations have scarpered.

P or C: We apologise for this our cock-up and declare that in place of this corpse we shall endeavour to invent something even more dumbed down and sham antique.

All: You can't be serious!

P or C: Oh yes, we can. Wait until you see Common Worship.

All: We don't believe it!

P or C: I don't blame you.

The following exorcism shall be read by a Real Anglican, a supporter of the Book of Common Prayer (1662); as it may be a churchwarden or some other such ploughman:

Ploughman: Thou deadly (and now dead) book, we would fain have clutched thee to our breast and loved thee for thy wisdom and thine own name's sake. But verily when we openest thee we perceived that thou wert full of vain things, neither hot nor cold but a striving after wind. Because thou art a vile thing, we therefore most heartily cast thee to the worms in the name of all that is well-appointed and agreeable to right doctrine.

Here followeth The Psalm

Like as the chaff is before the wind, and the frost before the morning:
　　　　So is the Alternative Service Book, altogether out of mind.
For lo, they said, there is nothing like unto it:
　　　　It shall light the generations and by it shall all men be blessed.
But lo, it passeth away even as a dream:
　　　　And no man can remember it.
We were told it was the bees' knees, though we found it ever so cheesy:
　　　　Therefore shall it enter the fire, and the land shall know it no more.
Glory, glory, we would rather
(Glory, glory, let's have fun):
Return rejoicing to the proper Prayer Book;
With imitations let's have done. A-person.

The Committal

The President (or Commissar) shall kneel before the Real Anglican and shall say:

I give you this box of matches as a sign of a roaring good fire.
The people, the Real Anglican preceding them, shall leave the church by the west door and walk in not too solemn procession...*

* One (or more) of the following acclamations may be shouted:

Good riddance! Rubbish! Let's be done with it!
...until they come nigh unto the pile of ASBs in the churchyard. When all is conveniently prepared, the Real Anglican shall say (or sing):
We do set this fire to show that we have passed from darkness to light. These two score years dwelt we in thick darkness, and behold it was exceeding thick. Now we do give thanks for that we are delivered from the plague of vain words and our sorrow is ended.
Kneeling before the pile of books he shall strike matches (as many as shall be required to kindle a blaze) while the people dancing shall sing the hymn following:

> The book they gave us now is burning,
> The flames leap upwards at our behest,
> And men of England are returning
> Again to the book that they love best.
>
> No longer obeying those tedious instructions
> To "turn to the prayer on page ninety-two",
> Or having to prattle pedestrian constructions
> Like "a guest at a wedding" and "also with you".
>
> Never again this "delight and tenderness"
> Or "responsibly and after serious thought";
> At last we have exorcised that sort of slenderness,
> Returned to repeating the words that we ought.

102

Confusing alternatives, various "sections"
And bishops preceding Her Majesty the Queen;
A sanitised litany, and NEB lections,
These are all things that had better not been.

Come let us make merry with dancing and singing,
It raises our spirits to see the flames leap;
"Long live the Real Prayer Book!" let church bells be ringing,
As two decades' rubbish lies burnt in a heap.
Tune: C.C.Scholefield (1839-1904)

Malmsey wine shall be served after the custom.

Let Us Now Praise Famous Men – and Women

St Michael's has long and distinguished musical connections, beginning with the visit of Henry Purcell who was first to play the organ at our church back in the 17th century. William Boyce – Handel's famous contemporary – was Master of the Music here for thirty-two years in the 18th century – until he was dismissed for habitual drunkenness. In 1864, the Royal College of Organists was founded at St Michael's by Richard Limpus.

But the most famous and best-loved of the musicians associated with our church is Harold Darke, who was organist from 1916 until 1966. During that time – including the war years and the Blitz – he gave a recital every Monday lunchtime in the world's longest running series of organ recitals. There are a few left who can still remember Harold as he stumbled through the rubble of bomb damage in 1940 and 1941. He wrote musical settings for Matins and Evensong, including the well-known Darke in F which, of course, is known to all church musicians as "effin' dark". His version of In The Bleak Midwinter – the magnificently evocative carol by Christina Rossetti – is sung every year at our carol service, and there is never a dry eye in the house.

I have already mentioned that Ralph Vaughan Williams used to conduct the St Michael's Singers. He died in 1958 and his name is in the Book of Remembrance in my other church of St Sepulchre, which is the National Musicians' Church. Vaughan Williams married late in life and his widow Ursula, now well into her nineties, lives in north London.

It was a pleasure and an honour to be invited to take afternoon tea with the great lady. I was shown upstairs to her sitting-room, where tea and scones were all set out on a silver tray in the traditional manner. Ursula, elegant, slender and bright-eyed, immediately began to tell stories about her late husband: how he had studied with Ravel; his attachment to the poetry of Walt Whitman; his dislike of Delius; his wide and various taste in music so that, she said, "He never wrote the same symphony twice – not like some composers I could name!" I'm rather glad she didn't!

Once, she recalled with glee, Vaughan Williams was coming home with Edward Elgar from some musicians' banquet somewhere in the City of London. They had dined and supped very well, as usual. They were walking past a particular house when they saw a man, looking worse for wear and lying in the doorway. Their replete and expansive mood made them feel quite charitable towards the old chap and so Elgar suggested, "Let's try the door and, if it's open, we'll put him inside out of the weather."

So the two composers struggled with the bulk of the fellow until they had him upstairs and on the bed. Feeling they had done their good deed for the day, they walked off down the street. They had gone only thirty or forty yards when a shout went up, "Oi!" and a little boy's face appeared at the window – "...that's not my dad!"

I don't think they turned round.

One winter evening, our musicians put on a performance of Haydn's The Creation at St Sepulchre's and Lady Vaughan Williams came with a friend. In the interval she asked if she might use the bathroom. I brought her through into the Rectory and asked if she'd like a drink of tea:

"Oh no, thank you."

"Coffee?"

"No, thank you – nothing to drink."

"Gin and tonic?"

"Yes, please – make mine a large one!"

It was a pleasure.

St Sepulchre's is always teeming with musicians, and in the millennium year the BBC Promenade Concerts season held its international press launch here. A well-wisher paid for the church to be thoroughly cleaned and all the chairs were moved to the sides, exposing the magnificent black and white squares which make up the floor of the vast nave. St Sepulchre's is the biggest church in the City of London. The choir of King's College Cambridge came, under their director Stephen Cleobury, and altogether it was a stupendous musical event broadcast worldwide.

It was entirely appropriate that the BBC Proms should launch the millennium season at St Sepulchre's, for the first Promenade Concerts were founded by Henry Wood in 1895 and Wood, as a boy, learnt the organ at our church. He was always an intense and highly energetic man and, when young, something of a prodigy – the sort of prodigy who irritates his music teacher.

Wood was an extrovert from the start – never backward at coming forward. From the moment when, aged two and straining to get a better sight of a hurdy-gurdy player and his monkey, he fell out of his baby chair and broke his nose, there was never any doubt that he would make his presence felt in the world. His character, even as a child, suggested highly nervous perpetual motion bordering on mania. He rigged up a communications system of pipes between his own room and that of his parents; and at night he stuffed a cork into his end of the pipe so that they wouldn't hear his insomniacal piano practice. By the side of his piano he kept white mice and a guinea pig, as well as an Alexander harmonium bought from Noel Coward's uncle.

There was no shortage of self-confidence. As a child, he met many renowned artists and musicians and he recorded these meetings in his diary: "Sir Arthur Sullivan asked my advice…Ruskin looked at me with interest." Even young Henry was not infallible though, and he confesses to having once played a funeral march at a wedding.

As I said, Sir Henry Wood's ashes are now interred in the north wall of the Musicians' Chapel in St Sepulchre's. There is a stained glass window in his honour: it features one picture of young Henry learning the organ and another of him in his pomp conducting a Promenade Concert at the Queen's Hall. There are also windows to the composer John Ireland and the Australian diva Dame Nellie Melba. At the north extremity of the Musicians' Chapel is a window in honour of Carroll, who wrote the song Nymphs and Shepherds which was famously recorded back in the 1940s by the Luton Girls' Choir. Underneath the Carroll window is a poetic inscription which includes the words, "All the virgins bear their parts" – which reportedly, regularly produced guffaws from the choirboys in the old days.

One morning, I was cleaning the candles on the high altar and enjoying the sunshine which in the late spring lights the church and makes it glow like a golden jewellery box. There were one or two visitors

106

wandering about the place. One of them came and asked me to tell him about a bell he had found on the pillar at the front of the nave on the south side.

"Oh, yes," I said. "That's the Execution Bell." And I drew his attention to the inscribed quotation from Macbeth underneath:

> "It was the owl that shrieked, the fatal bellman,
> Which gives the stern'st goodnight."

Shakespeare used often to travel along Holborn, past St Sepulchre's, and he must have witnessed the grim scene of the condemned man being taken from Newgate Prison, just across the road, put in the cart and driven to be hanged at Tyburn. I said, "Shakespeare would have heard the bell, too. It was rung by our Sexton who, on the night before an execution, would make his way along an underground passage which led from St Sepulchre's into the jail."

Upon receiving this information, my visitor turned the colour of a newly-starched surplice and ran out of church without another word. And before I had time to explain that the phrases "in the cart" – meaning in deep trouble – and "going west" – being on the way out – derive from those macabre events.

There is always a small crowd of tourists gazing up at another of our attractions: the window in memory of John Smith, the first Governor of the Commonwealth of Virginia in the United States. Smith was born in our parish and grew up to be an adventurer – some would say a pirate. In 1607, he set sail in three tiny ships and founded the Virginian Colony, of which he became first governor. Walt Disney tells the rest of the story – and tells it wrongly. Smith was indeed captured by Indians and rescued by the Princess Pocahontas. But she did not marry him: she married one of his men, returned with him to England and died of a fever at Gravesend.

The Rector of St Michael's:
"A Conman Operating a Scam"

It's not difficult for a City Rector to provoke a scandal. St Michael's is a Grade I listed building and, since parish churches get no financial help from the state, we are always struggling to maintain the fabric and pay our way. This is not easy, as we have no resident population in the City. So we decided to levy the Voluntary Rate – a statute dating from 1956 which allows churches to render an annual account to the businesses within their parishes. It's called "voluntary" because, while we are allowed to levy it, the businesses are not obliged to pay it.

Hoping to benefit from the festive spirit, we sent out our levy in the week before Christmas. Although City parishes have been sending out voluntary rate demands for years, for some reason our levy captured the interest of the press. A journalist on the City pages of The Times phoned me for further information and then printed what, for me at least, was a very gratefully received three paragraphs about St Michael's. The other broadsheets, picking up from The Times' piece, followed with short and friendly articles of their own. One even printed a highly flattering colour photograph of me in my vestments standing on the church steps!

I was glad to be able to report to the Churchwardens that, by the end of January, we had received about £10,000. I supposed that not every business would pay the rate in full. Many phoned to say they would prefer to make a donation instead. Fine by me: all contributions gratefully received. But the point is that none of the companies in our parish showed us any hostility; no one actually objected to the levy. There was only one sour note and it came from that dour band of atheistical Calvinists, the national Secular Society: people for whom jokes are no laughing matter. They bridled at the thought that God might be gaining something from Mammon. Well, that's fair enough: live and let live. No one is forced to pay the voluntary rate - and no one is forced to believe in God. Though I recall a telling piece of graffiti which said, "God is dead – Nietzsche", and then printed the reply, "Nietzsche is dead – God".

But it was the manner of the NSS' objection that struck me as petulant and dishonest: they issued a press release which accused me, by
name, of being a "conman" and operating "a scam". This was too much
for even that repository of political correctness, the BBC. They sent a
bright young reporter round to interview me for the Today programme.
He began by asking me what I thought of the NSS' response. I said,
"Well, it's not very nice, is it? I mean when an Englishman acting
entirely within his legal rights is accused of being a conman operating
a scam, it's a bit much."

He asked me, "How angry do you feel towards them?"

I replied, "Speaking not as a petulant atheist, but as a Christian, naturally I forgave them instantly."

"Don't you think your letter levying the rate might be misleading
and browbeat businesses into thinking the rate is compulsory – that
you might confuse people?"

I said, "Are you suggesting that stockbrokers and insurance agents,
responsible for handling billions of pounds every day of the week,
can't read and that they don't know the difference between 'voluntary'
and 'compulsory'? Besides, the idea that an ordinary parish priest
might financially bamboozle all those high-flying City slickers beg-
gars belief."

They are an interesting anachronism, the NSS, and a worthwhile
subject for forensic study: a splendidly fossilised example of the philo-
sophically discredited materialism of the Victorian age. Their motto is,
"To be on the side of rationality, intelligence and decency". Well, St
Thomas Aquinas and Albert Einstein didn't think it irrational or unin-
telligent to believe in God. And, when it comes to decency, they
weren't very decent when they started calling me names unjustly, were
they?

The list of prominent members of the NSS features many of the
usual high-minded suspects: among others, Sir Michael Foot, Richard
Dawkins, Alice Mahon, Polly Toynbee, Harold Pinter and Sir Ludovic
Kennedy. By their utterances ye shall know them. I remember reading
an article some years ago by Polly Toynbee, that mistress of the non
sequitur, in which she blamed God for the death of her colleague on
The Guardian Jill Tweedie; then went on to say that, but of course, she,
Toynbee, didn't believe in God.

I'd love to attend the AGM of the NSS. I imagine Michael Foot asleep in his donkey jacket, while Ludovic Kennedy says, "When we're old, we should have the right to kill ourselves." And Alice Mahon replying, "We're all old. Let's kill ourselves now."

At this point Richard Dawkins, wearing a genetically determined pained expression, asks, "But how shall we do it?"

In fractured grammar and after an agonising pause, Harold Pinter says, "I know: let's bore ourselves to death!"

No, but satire is impossible faced with this dreary bunch of inadvertent comedians. Here is what they are up to for real. I have just been looking into their latest stunt which they call "Heroes of Atheism". Members are being invited to nominate their favourite atheist and, when the votes are counted, the face of the winning atheist will be imprinted on the official NSS pottery. A mug-shot for mugs, you might say.

But guess who is threatening to top the poll? Not Tom Paine or David Hume or Sigmund Freud, but the Theosophical nutter Annie Besant. She was a devotee of the Higher Hampstead Buddhism, and she once said, at a meeting attended by G.K. Chesterton, "There is no such thing as right or wrong, good or evil; just the gentle upwards drift of the universe."

To which Chesterton replied, "If there's no such thing as right or wrong, good or evil, how does she know there's such a thing as up or down?"

Now there's a remark that is truly rational, intelligent and decent. It is also - something of which the moth-eaten atheists of the NSS are utterly incapable – humorous.

For The Fallen

It was the most sickening moment in my years at St Michael's. I went into church one morning to find that the Regimental Colours of the Stock Exchange Branch of the Royal Fusiliers had been ripped from their pole in the nave and stolen. The Colours had hung in our church since 1919. You couldn't have a more poignant memorial: underneath where the Colours hung are two glass cases containing the names of the men who fell in the First World War: more than three hundred – and they from just one battalion. I often think we lack a sense of proportion, that we live attenuated, effete lives these days – especially when, for example, we read that the journalists who went across to Normandy to commemorate the D-Day landings were offered counselling. The soldiers who actually went across in 1944 and did the job received no counselling; but then they wouldn't have asked for it.

St Sepulchre's is proud of a larger military tradition. At the west end of the church, on the north side, there is a monument to the 6th Battalion, the London Rifles and the names of their campaigns are inscribed prominently on a wooden screen. What thoughts and feelings arise when you walk into church on a winter's morning and read: "St Quentin ... Loos ... Amiens ... Pursuit to Mons ... Passchendaele ... Somme ... Ypres ... Menin Road"?

Close by there is a wooden cross, dilapidated now, almost rotted away. It was taken from the battlefield at the Battle of Loos, where for three years it commemorated the one hundred officers and men of the 6th Battalion, the London Regiment who fell there on 25th September, 1918.

St Sepulchre's is the church of the Royal Regiment of Fusiliers and the whole of the south wall is decorated with the names of deceased Fusiliers. Over the south aisle hang the Regiment's Battle Colours for many campaigns – some as long ago as Portugal in the 18th century. Most are bedraggled now, fretted as a moth frets a garment. But that just serves to remind visitors of the true saying that old soldiers never die, but only fade away.

They do not fade from our recollection, though. Their footfalls echo

111

in the memory. Every year on Remembrance Sunday they come to St Sepulchre's for their Service of Remembrance: cadets, veterans, serving officers and men – upwards of three hundred soldiers in church. First, they parade by their memorial half a mile away at Holborn Bar. Such evocation in the November half-light: melancholy, heroic, but the atmosphere throughout suffused with the supreme sense of comradeship and sacrifice. The Last Post, the veterans wearing their campaign medals, the cadets eager and immaculate. The antique drum and the march from the memorial to the church.

I have heard some lousy sermons on Remembrance Sunday from clergy who speak only of "the horror of war". Yes, war is horrible, but this is part of what I said when it was my turn to preach last year. I wanted above all to try to show that war involves not just nations but ordinary men – extraordinary men – of flesh and blood. There are human stories here. Frankly, I was sick of all those ungrateful sermons which talk down the soldier's calling. I wanted to thank them for what they did for us...

"Just over fifty years ago, on 9th June, 1952, the First Battalion of the Royal Fusiliers, under the command of Lt Colonel Dick Stevens marched through the City of London, past the Lord Mayor, on their way to lunch at the Guildhall. A fortnight later they sailed from Liverpool in the ship The Empire Halladale to join the war in Korea.

"When they arrived in the Far East six weeks later, Major Terry Donnelly, commanding C Company of mainly Cockney Fusiliers, joked with his men, 'With a ladder and some glasses you could see the Hackney Marshes, if it wasn't for the houses in between.'

"The Korean War at this stage was mainly a night-time campaign with patrols creeping through the minefields to gather information. By day the soldiers lived a troglodyte existence in a maze of trenches. The major operation involving the battalion was OP PIMLICO. On the night of 24th November, 1952, D Company, commanded by Major Mike Chard, were ambushed by a large Chinese force after they had set out to raid enemy lines. Great heroism was displayed by all the Company, but still fourteen were killed, nineteen wounded and eight taken prisoner. Fusilier George Hodkinson, the wireless operator who had taken command when Kit Hoare and all the NCOs had been knocked out, was awarded the Distinguished Conduct Medal for his

112

deeds on that night. Before being taken prisoner, and in spite of his wounds, George had calmly reported the battle over the radio and called down artillery and mortar fire on the enemy. His final words before capture were, 'This is it. They are coming again in strength. We shall be overrun this time. Nothing can stop them now.'

"Early 1953 saw the battalion in Corps reserve but they were soon back in the line again. In late May, the Duke of Wellington's Regiment, on the key strategic position of the Hook, were attacked in force. Ten thousand shells landed on their position on one night alone. The Fusiliers were ordered up to support the Dukes and they took over the hill on 29th May. The Hook battle took place at the same time as the climbing of Mount Everest and the Coronation of Elizabeth II, so there were very few reports back home in the press. But this battle was a major factor in contributing to the armistice which followed two months later. This is yet another example of Korea as 'the forgotten war'. And it was not until 1987 that a memorial to those who fell was dedicated by the Queen in St Paul's.

"Now, I have never been a soldier. But my father served in the RAF during the Second World War and my father-in-law at El Alamein. I have numbered soldiers, sailors and airmen among my dearest friends and colleagues all through my career. In all this time, I have never met a soldier who wanted to go to war. Yet every soldier I have had the honour to meet always knew the truth of Edmund Burke's saying: 'The only thing necessary for the triumph of evil is for good men to do nothing.'

"And I have been sickened in my lifetime to see how Remembrance Sunday has been hijacked in the schools and in the churches by pacifists. The only poetry that gets read is the maudlin, cowardly stuff by Wilfred Owen. And in most places, the prayers are always about the horror of war and the evil of war. Now every soldier knows more than these armchair politicos about the horror of war and the evil of war. But what the soldier also knows is that there are worse evils than warfare. Worse than warfare is non-resistance in the face of the aggressor who would kill or enslave you, your family, our nation.

"I spent a good part of my ministry in Yorkshire, and so I had plenty of opportunity to get acquainted with the York Quaker pacifist ladies. Let me tell you: this sort is not harmless; they are not merely

113

picturesque, quaint, high-minded eccentrics. Pacifism is the enemy of peace, because it is the enemy of justice and righteousness. For pacifism always prefers the triumph of evil to necessary resistance. Pacifism and the appeasement of the aggressor always lead to more trouble in the long run. If the governments of the allied nations had listened to Churchill, Harold Nicholson and Duff Cooper in the 1930s instead of to the treacherous Lord Halifax and the lying Rab Butler, Hitler could have been stopped in his tracks and millions of lives would have been saved.

"And a lot of modern churchmen forget that Christ who said, 'Blessed are the peacemakers' also said, 'I come not to send peace but a sword'. I am tired of having to listen to the slander by those clergymen and school-teachers who make up today's liberal establishment in which they speak of patriotism, the love of one's country and the willingness to lay down one's life as 'jingoism'. I cannot abide the fact that the memory of our valiant dead is ungratefully insulted in this way.

"Here, from the First World War, is a memory of two soldiers from the seventh battalion of the Northumberland Fusiliers:

Private Bob Young was conscious right to the end. I lay alongside him and said, "Can I do anything for you, Bob?" He said, "Straighten my legs, Jack." But he had no legs. He said, "Get my wife's photograph out of my breast pocket." I took the photograph out and put it in his hands. He couldn't move. He couldn't lift a hand. He couldn't lift a finger. But he somehow held his wife's photograph on his chest. And that's how Bob Young died.

"In short, the Christian believes that death is not the worst thing that can happen: worse, far worse, than death is the triumph of wrong. This is why the Thirty-Nine Articles of Religion in the Book of Common Prayer – Articles which all the clergy, including Dr Williams, are obliged to recite and affirm – contain these words: 'It is lawful for Christian men, at the commandment of the Magistrate, to wear weapons and serve in the wars.'

"May God bless you all and all those who serve in our armed forces."

One day I was asked to preach at St Lawrence Jewry, the famous old church by the Guildhall and the one used by the Lord Mayor and the Corporation of London for ceremonials. My address was to the veterans of the war in Japan.

Afterwards, at the reception, I met a man called Neil Boyd. In the Second World War he was plucked out of the western desert and sent to fight in the Far East, where he was captured by the Japanese. He was kept half-starved in a cage underground and the passing soldiers urinated and defecated on him. Occasionally he was taken out and tortured. This continued for two years, then one morning he was put on a train. He hadn't a clue where he was being taken. Well, it turned out to be Hiroshima. As he told me:

"It was a morning of the most brilliant blue. I was awoken out of my dozing by a Japanese soldier jumping up and down, shouting and pointing at the sky. Suddenly a series of explosions rent the air and it seemed the whole universe was splitting apart. Fearful and brilliant colours, the like of which I had never seen before, like an evil blossom enveloping me...

"It was like watching my own death. The mists and darkness began to clear a little. I was blind in one eye, with only dim sight in the other. In this pitiful state, I began to look for my companion and fellow prisoner. All that was left of him was a shadowy imprint on the tower wall. And the tower was the only thing standing except for two factory chimneys in the distance. I had survived only because I had been sheltered by that wall and lying down...

"A ship of the US navy took me to San Francisco where the liberated American prisoners were treated like heroes. The few English were incarcerated in an open prison while they waited to decide what to do with us. I weighed just over five stone. I thought, I'm damned if I'm going to swap the Jap prison for a Yankee jail. So I escaped and worked my way across the States to New York, earning a sparse living by working on garage forecourts. The food I received was a banquet to what I had survived on in Japan."

Well, it's a long story but eventually Neil got to London and a train from King's Cross to Hull where he found that his street had been bombed and all his family were dead. He moved to York and took up painting - paintings which are startlingly evocative of his half-life in the camps. He also wrote a magnificent autobiography, An Englishman's Peace and War. Finally, he said, "I went back to Japan and asked Japanese soldiers how they could inflict such torture on their

115

captives. Japanese statesmen and politicians have apologised to me."

What Neil Boyd has received in his life could hardly be described as justice, but his parting shot to me was, "God is merciful."

The Royal Fusiliers have their headquarters at the Tower of London and I visit them for lunch now and then. It's good to go late in the evening, too, and watch the Ceremony of the Keys. The footsteps of the guard over the cobbles in that historic place – not so bloody as its reputation though, since only seven people were ever executed there.

"Halt! Who goes there?"

"The keys."

"Whose keys?"

"Queen Elizabeth's keys".

Footfalls echo in the memory.

In The Scrubs

Jail. Prison visiting. It's not so much the smell as the noise. Prisons are metallic places where everyone shouts. But you can hardly hear the shouting above the clanging. It's as if everything is taking place inside a big tin box. The jail is a cruel place. I have listened to convicted child-molesters protesting their love of children and registering their outrage upon being repeatedly beaten up by their fellow inmates who regard sex criminals as beneath contempt. There is a hierarchy among convicts – just as there is a hierarchy among the clergy. At the top, the murderers and gangsters, with the ordinary thieves and burglars the middle-rankers, so to speak. Fraudsters are looked down upon as mere pen-pushers. But everyone needs to think someone somewhere is worse than himself, so they all despise the child-molester.

Are there any limits to self-deceit? I was "given the form" – brought up to date concerning his criminal record – of a paedophile. He was a balding man, with what little hair he had left a distinguished grey. Neat. Compact. An open, kindly face. You might have taken him for a scientist or a doctor on the edge of retirement. He had for thirty years abused little girls – any child over the age of two might be his victim. His method was to give them sweets and presents and then rape them – or use his screwdrivers on them – and then get them to draw their childish pictures of the event. There is little one can imagine more obscene than the crude sex words written in a childish scrawl.

He said he wanted to talk to me, "to put the record straight". He was under the unswerving impression that he had never done anything wrong. He sat there with his arms folded and sipped at a cup of tea: "They lead you on, you know, Padre. Little mistresses, they are. I never meant any harm – just touching. I loved them all, you see." His face was scarred where the other inmates had razored him. He looked wary, glanced around him all the time we talked, like a small animal watching out for predators. For all his cruelty, he was pathetic, banal. As I walked back to the front desk, I thought it was not for nothing that St Thomas Aquinas said, "Evil is banal." An assistant governor told me afterwards, "He'll never be let out. He was convicted on eight counts, and God only knows how many more kids he's ruined. He had a stash of pornography bigger than the stack in the British Library."

From the pathetic to the tragic. I met a man in his sixties who was in for life. He was relaxed, nonchalant, eloquent. In his quiet voice he said, "She nagged me for years. Wouldn't let go. Like a dog worrying a rat, she was. I'm the rat. One day I just snapped and throttled her. I loved her. Still do. I'll be seventy-five when they let me out – if I'm lucky. And she won't be there for me."

Well, there's no doubt murder is wrong, but I felt sorry for him in a way I could not have felt sorry for the child-molester. The murder he had committed was a tragedy for him as well as for his wife. The noise of the jail. And the atmosphere oppressive, threatening, always it seems on the edge of exploding. I think it's a lot to do with the way the prison officers line the walls during free association, making it very obvious that they are armed with huge, ugly batons. And the inmates, watchful, resentful, restless. There is no peace. There is no ordinary relaxed time – even in those free association periods. Everyone is on edge. From time to time the inmates are rounded up – it might be for a meal, for work or locking up – and they slouch to where they are bidden with a mute contempt for the prison officers. They go to wherever they have to go as if they are doing so entirely of their own free will – as if the prison officers are not there at all.

One Sunday I was invited to take the Holy Communion Service in the prison chapel. About eighty men turned up. Most of them sat leaning forward slightly as an act of reverence. There were no kneelers. The organ struck up with Praise My Soul The King of Heaven and they sang lustily, if not tunefully. It was again dismaying to see the prison officers lining the walls. But, as the assistant governor replied afterwards, when I asked him if such a strong presence was really needed: "Well, Rector, how would you like to live dangerously? You had fourteen murderers in there."

I preached on the mercy of God and took as my text Psalm 56:8. "Thou tellest my wanderings: put thou my tears into thy bottle: are they not in thy book?" There was no need to try to "explain" the imagery – there never is, and those who try always end up ruining the effect. Many of the men were obviously mesmerised by those words. At the Communion, about half of them came forward to receive the Sacrament, but once again their movements were accompanied by an uneasy shuffle on the part of the officers.

After the service some stayed behind to talk. One – he looked no more than a boy – said, "You know what, Father? It's boring in here. It's boring – that's the trouble. I ain't gonna come back in here no more when I gets out. It's so boring. Just boring."

The wife-murderer hung about when the rest of them had gone, so that the officers came across and told him to leave: "The Padre has to go now." It was obvious they wanted all the inmates back in their cells before the next mealtime.

I said, "I'm in no great rush."

He had such a sorrowful, languid look. I said, "Is there anything I can do?"

"You've already done it. Those words. Will you tell me where I can find them? It'll be my prayer every night. So tender, you see – the idea that God has a bottle for our tears. So tender. I used to feel like that about my wife. Still do."

He turned and walked away slowly down the wide corridor that led to the cells. The only prison officer left in the Chapel gave me a look, then he followed the wife-murderer down the corridor, talking to him as if the two of them were old pals. I stood and looked towards the altar for a moment, then folded my surplice and headed for the security clearance desk and a late lunch.

Gaffes, Graces and Princes

When I arrived in the City in 1998, I was thrilled to be asked to be Chaplain to the Guild of Air Pilots and Air Navigators. I always enjoy my connection with the Guild because its members – for all their technical know-how and professional skill - are practical, hands-on, down to earth types and they wear their expertise lightly. There's no bullshit – and you wouldn't expect any from seasoned RAF and commercial airmen. One Sunday, for example, the Lay Sheriff of London, a pilot and a member of the Guild, turned up for Choral Evensong a little late: "Sorry, Rector, I've just been having a spin in a Spitfire."

They like a joke, too. So it was both a mark of genius and most happy fate that the Duke of Edinburgh long since agreed to become their Grand Master. In 1958, Prince Philip, in characteristic style, assured the Lord Mayor that the Guild would not present an automatic pilot for admission to Freedom of the City until the Lord Mayor's chair was occupied by a robed robot.

I wonder if any guild or association of tradesmen has ever in the field of human endeavour had to counter so much scepticism and plain ridicule as the aviators? And not just from ignorant peasants, either. A handful of years before the first flight, Lord Kelvin, President of the Royal Society, announced: Heavier than air flying machines are impossible. I have not the smallest molecule of faith in aerial navigation other than ballooning. The Harvard professor William Pickering wrote in Aeronautics magazine in 1908: A popular fallacy is to expect enormous speeds to be obtained. There is no hope of competing for racing speed with either our locomotives or our automobiles. I think my favourite is from the National Academy of Sciences Committee on Gas Turbines, in June 1940: "The so called jet engine can hardly be considered a feasible application to air frames." Having been working on jet propulsion for ten years, Frank Whittle replied: "Good thing I was too stupid to know this."

Typically forthright words from an airman! Having now been to dozens of Guild Court meeting and banquets, I can testify that all the legends about the airman's fondness for laconically dicing with death are true. At one of the first dinners I attended I met the Junior Warden: "junior" does not refer to his age – he was sixtyish – but to the usual hierarchy in livery companies: Junior Warden becomes Senior Warden and then, a year later, Master. We were well into the champagne after a long Court meeting. The Junior Warden, I noticed, spoke in an extremely gravelly voice, as if he had a bad dose of laryngitis. He said, "I know what you're thinking, Peter. You think I've got some horrible disease, don't you? Well, I haven't. I talk like this because I had a bit of a prang some years ago when I was the bloke who trained the test pilots on the Harrier Jump Jet."

"Who trained you?"

Talk about laconic. "Oh they sent me up with the manual on my knee. Anyhow, I had to eject at 35,000 feet. Got out of the plane all right. Trouble was, I took half of the cockpit with me. Broke quite a lot of bones. It was months before I was up in the sky again."

It was then that I saw a man standing by himself in the corner. Remembering the etiquette about seeing that no one is left out, I went over to have a word. He looked rather distinguished and about sixty-five, I thought. Knowing that all members of the Guild are or were hands-on pilots or navigators in the RAF or with commercial airlines, I asked innocently – too innocently as it turned out – "Were you a commercial pilot or in the RAF?"

"Oh, I'm still in the RAF."

Well, I ought to have been warned, oughtn't I? But, like a man digging his own grave, I pressed on: "What is it exactly that you do?"

"Actually, I'm Air Chief Marshal Bowering."

Only the head of the RAF, the whole damned shoot! His companion covered my discomfiture with a sudden joke:

This plane's going to New York, you see. There's a blonde airhead sitting in a seat she shouldn't be sitting in at the front. So the steward goes over to her and says, "Excuse me, Miss, but this seat is taken by a VIP who happens to be talking with the pilot on the flight deck just now. Allow me to escort you to one further back."

The blonde will have none of it. She says, "I'm a blonde and I'm smart and I'm going to New York." The steward's protestations are to no avail. So he calls the chief steward who goes through the same procedure, with the same result: "I'm a blonde and I'm smart and I'm going to New York."

All the stewards are out of their minds with frustration – and the VIP will be back wanting his seat in a minute. They're surprised then when shortly afterwards they see the blonde has retreated to a seat near the back. Whereupon the pilot appears with a smirk all across his face: "I got her to move!"

"How the hell did you do that, sir?"

"Well, she came out with her spiel, 'I'm a blonde and I'm smart and I'm going to New York.' So I told her, 'The front end of the plane isn't going to New York.'"

Nonchalance is the pilot's trademark. After dinner, one of the airline pilots told me that, "...bringing home an empty plane 30,000 feet over Nova Scotia," a window broke – not the whole thing or otherwise the cabin would have been catastrophically depressurised – but the outer was shattered, leaving only a thin shield. "I brought the speed right down and lost some height. We made it OK – though I'm afraid we were a bit behind schedule."

You get outings with the Guild and one of the most thrilling was a day-long visit to the wartime RAF Fighter Command's underground bunker operations room at Uxbridge. This was where the invading Luftwaffe, plotted on radar, were represented by counters pushed around on the central table: "Bandits four hundred. Angels One-Five." Above was the gallery where Winston Churchill sat when he visited on 15th September, 1940, on the climactic day of the Battle of Britain and asked, "How many reserves have we?"

"We have none, Sir."

At Uxbridge, I met some of the pilots from that battle: elegant gentlemen in their seventies and eighties, their whole demeanour understatement. One said, "I was nineteen and in a Spitfire squadron. On my first combat mission I came out of the clouds and saw three or four hundred Nazi bombers aiming for London. I must admit I gulped a bit, as there were only eight of us. Soon cheered up though when our squadron leader came over the radio and said, 'Come on boys, let's surround the bastards!'"

They ask me to say Grace at Guild Banquets, and so far I have had no complaints about undue "levity" from Past Masters. On the contrary, the men would very likely take me out and shoot me if I were to utter anything drab. So, for the New Year Court Dinner at the RAF Club:

Bold airmen stand o'er all the earth,

Post Christmas cheer, extended girth;
This evening there's no chance we might
Try losing weight or gaining height:
So we who hurtle through the skies
Look forward to more chips and pies.   Amen.

And for the Banquet in Merchant Taylors' Hall after the Annual Service:

There was a famous airman,
His wings they gleamed like brass;
He fell out of his cockpit
And landed in a tree.
He said, "My word, I'm lucky -
Thank God that I'm still here!"
So we raise our hearty thanks
For all this evening's cheer. Amen.

For the Trophies and Awards Dinner, when prizes are presented for outstanding achievements in flight or navigation:

The airman's lot is all delight:
He flies by day, he flies by night;
He trails his wings above the cloud
And as he soars he thinks aloud:
"Just wait till I'm back on the deck,
I'll eat like a horse and drink like heck;
But, drunk or sober or full to the brim,
I'll remember to raise my thanks to Him."

Her Majesty the Queen has been Patron of the Guild for fifty years and Prince Philip our Grand Master for the same length of time. The Queen let it be known that, after such a stint, she would rather like to retire. Prince Philip generously agreed to be our new Patron and we were delighted when his son Prince Andrew stepped into his father's shoes and took on the role of Grand Master. Of course, we held a Court meeting followed by a dinner to ratify the new arrangements.

The Wardens, Clerk and Chaplain gathered in a small room in the

RAF Club to welcome the Princes. Philip came in, his hands behind his back and a great grin on his face. When he saw the Wardens in their blue fur and livery he exclaimed, "Ah, medieval airmen!" He shook hands with us all and so did Andrew; then within minutes – since both Philip and Andrew are experienced pilots – the conversation was all the usual banter about flying at nought feet over the sea without instruments or lights. When it came to dinner time, I had to stand beside Prince Philip and say Grace. I thought it was probably not an occasion for the usual sort of thing, but perhaps something a little more…well, princely. So I cobbled together a little pretend King James Version, something a bit like an Old Testament Psalm:

> Bring forth the best wine;
> Let thy table be decked with all good things:
> For the Prince is come in,
> The Prince is come in, O Lord
> Even unto the great feast.
> Let all the company rejoice
> And be exceeding glad. Amen.

Philip leaned across and whispered enquiringly, "Isaiah?"

And I'm afraid to say that I had the temerity to reply, "One eye's higher than the other, Sir!"

Once Grace had been said and the doors closed, the two Princes were the very spirit of the party with airmen's jokes and banter until midnight.

The Guild of Air Pilots and Air Navigators has provided me with some of the most enjoyable nights out during the whole of my time in the City. The Guild was founded at Rules restaurant, Covent Garden, in 1929, but there was an early shocking setback when the Master and Deputy Master perished in the Airship R.101 disaster. The Guild became associated with St Michael's in 1957 and they have come to our church for their Annual Service ever since. At the end of his excellent History of the Guild, David Brown has written some moving words about this long association:

"Flying tends to breed a philosophy of its own. In the beginning, from the time when the landscape first expands beneath the wings after take-off, and earth-bound humans shrink to insignificance, there is a sense of pride and freedom. Later, as experience is gained, there comes a more lasting sense of detachment, and pride gives way gradually to humility born of the realisation of human limitations in the face of the elements, and of a working environment which, by day and night, can be at times forbidding and at other times overwhelmingly beautiful – and sometimes both."

What Have the Livery Companies Ever Done for Us?

As the Worshipful Company of Woolmen never tire of telling me, wool dominated English and European history for centuries, to a degree scarcely imaginable in our more synthetic, automated times. For instance, when in the Crusades, Richard the Lionheart was ransomed abroad, the ransom was paid in wool. Wool was the currency for hundreds of years. The very Chancellor plumps himself down on a woolsack. Actually, it's not so long ago that it was discovered the sack was filled with straw. It was the Woolmen's Company who got rid of the straw and replaced it with wool – once called "this sovereign merchandise and jewel of the realm".

The Woolmen are an ancient and noble Guild with a distinguished history. But it has to be reported that they did not always behave themselves. In 1180, King Henry II fined them for operating without a licence. And the first London Bridge was paid for out of a wool tax, so giving rise to the legend that the foundations of the bridge were built on woolpacks. In the nursery rhyme Baa Baa Black Sheep, the "three bags full" refers to an ancient wool export tax.

The legend also runs that one of the privileges of being made a Freeman of the City of London is that you are allowed to drive your sheep over London Bridge. I haven't seen many flocks recently.

At times, the wool trade slumped and quite extreme measures were taken to revive it. For example, Charles II decreed that all shrouds should be made from wool, prompting Alexander Pope's verse protest:

> 'Odious is woollen! T'would a saint provoke'
> Were the last words that poor Narissa spoke;
> 'No, let a charming chintz and Brussels lace
> Wrap my cold limbs and shade my lifeless face.'

Pretty Narissa would have been warmer in wool.

And in 1685, the House of Commons passed a bill requiring women to wear woollen hats.

There is an ancient connection between the wool trade and Cornhill, the parish of St Michael's. The City Coffee House used to organise wool sales "by the candle". This is how it was done: a candle, studded with pins at regular intervals, was lit and wool offered for auction. The last bid before a pin dropped secured the lot of wool on offer.

The Company's modern connection with St Michael's goes back to 1973 and my predecessor, the Reverend Norman Motley, who held the first Woolmen's Annual Service here.

Wool has penetrated to the very centre of our speech and language. If a person is out and out, we call him "dyed in the wool". If I am deceived, I have had "the wool pulled over my eyes". If you take a man's money, you "fleece him". Or you may be kept "on tenterhooks". We might go in for "wool-gathering" - but not, I hope, during a sermon. And the bride to be, of course, is called a "spinster".

I confess I was terrified, full of fear and trembling, at the prospect of coming to work in the City of London. When I was up in Yorkshire, waiting for the various interviews for my job as Rector of St Michael's, I was made more nervous by the sorts of advice I was given by people I suppose I should describe as well-wishers. One of them took me to one side and said, "You'll find the City of London completely nerve-wracking. It's all protocol and form. And the slightest word out of place – even the hint of a smile when you shouldn't – and you're marked for life."

As I sat on the train on the way to the big City, that friend's words smouldered in my ears and, by the time we'd reached Peterborough, I was all for getting off and going back home. I began to wish I had the gift of the mot juste, that mastery of protocol I have often observed by which the gifted socialite can move with effortless grace among princes and peasants alike.

But my first encounter with a City of London livery company turned out to be a very agreeable occasion: it was lunch at Drapers' Hall – the Drapers being our Patrons at St Michael's. They were all delightful and my table manners must have been fairly acceptable after all, for I am still here today.

The ease which one feels in such as the Worshipful Company of Fuellers comes mainly through the knowledge that this is another of those hands-on organisations: members actually know something

about the real, physical world – in this case the world of energy supply, whether it be coal, oil, gas or whatever.

Another company which comes to St Michael's for an Annual
Service is the Worshipful Company of Water Conservators. I'm not a
member of their livery, but I must say I think of myself as an honourable associate or fellow-traveller, having done as much as possible
to conserve water in my time by drinking very little of it. At first
glance, environmental preservation doesn't sound like the most exciting preoccupation – unlike, say, lion-taming or chartered accountancy.
I remember it was Mrs Thatcher – as she was then – who said in 1982
at the height of the Falklands War, "It's exciting to have a real life crisis on your hands, when you've spent half your political life dealing
with humdrum things like the environment." Hmm. One might feel
like replying to the effect that the landscape of our home country is
every bit as important as a parcel of land on the other side of the world.

Members of the Water Conservators enjoy adventures. I'm intrigued
by the sound of their annual commemoration on 14th July of Richard
I's handing over care of the Thames to the Corporation of London; and
of how this still involves every year the presentation of a glass jug of
Thames water to the Lord Mayor who certifies it fit to drink. No Lord
Mayor has yet dropped dead on the quay.

The Company enjoys colourful celebrations – such as their float at
the Lord Mayor's Show, with liverymen carrying water buckets
(empty, thank goodness) and their daughters and granddaughters
dressed as teardrops. One year, Master and Clerk, following Thomas
Platter's historic example in the 17th century, were rowed from the
Festival Pier to the Globe theatre for a performance of Julius Caesar.
In the year 2000, the Master made the noble boast, "All water used for
flushing toilets at the Millennium Dome was reclaimed."

Visiting Speakers

I try to make sure that the congregation doesn't have to listen to me and my sermons every week and so, from the first, I have invited visiting speakers. The generosity of these superstars has surprised me – though I'm sure it should not have. Every one of them turned down the fee offered. One of the first of the luminaries to address us was Professor John Macquarrie, the distinguished theologian who has won every honour there is for his work and thought. I was nervous about inviting him, for he had been one of the great intellectuals heroes of my youth. When I was training for the ministry, I was dismissive of the orthodoxy taught at the theological college and I assumed, as young students often do, that there was some superior wisdom which my tutors were missing.

It was then that I found John Macquarrie's book An Existentialist Theology, a comparison of the secular philosopher Martin Heidegger and the radical Christian theologian Rudolf Bultmann. It was full of stuff to delight young rebels: jargonistic phrases such as "inauthentic existence"; "being for" and "being that" – really just the fashionable vocabulary for a youngster like me, brought up on films from the French New Wave, trendy coffee bars, Espresso Bongo, the heavy eyelids of Juliet Greco, Gauloises cigarettes and Jean Paul-Sartre's apparently shocking statements such as, "It is unfortunate for existentialists that God does not happen to exist" and "Hell is other people." After forty years, one winces at one's own insouciance.

Of course, John Macquarrie had moved a long way from what he wrote in that early book and he came to us as an eminence and as one who had demonstrated throughout his life's work that it is not the trendy stuff but traditional thought that is really exciting. A tiny Scotsman in his eighties, wearing a beret and a luminous smile. A sizeable congregation had turned up to hear him. He began in his delicate, mellifluous Highland accent with a statement as radical, yet as orthodox as anyone – including St Augustine – might hope to hear: "God does not exist. It is God who allows whatever exists to exist." Words of authority articulated with the greatest diffidence. I'm convinced that if more people – especially the atheists and agnostics who run the Religious Affairs department at the

BBC - would listen to what is actually being said by theologians like John Macquarrie, they would not be so eager to dismiss traditional Christianity as "outdated". I took John to the City University Club for lunch and he related his experiences as a lifelong theologian with the sort of verve you might expect from the memoirs of an explorer of darkest Africa.

Over the port – though John had a wee dram instead – I made the elementary mistake of asking a rather nebulous question: "D'you think it would ever be possible to reconcile the sort of thinking in your An Existentialist Theology with the more traditional, scholastic thought?"

From the depth of his eighty-odd years' deep rumination on these issues, he replied with enormous courtesy and the broadest grin: "Oh, I should think so. I should certainly hope so. Why don't you do it?"

Never invite your heroes to come and speak to your people. You will be bound to mismanage the occasion out of a mixture of nervousness and awe. If that happened to me, to a degree, with Professor Macquarrie, it happened with a much greater severity when I asked Michael Brearley to come and talk to us. After he retired from being England's most successful cricket captain since the war, Michael trained as a psychoanalyst and he now practises his Freudian methods in Hampstead.

Recalling his superlative cricketing tactics, I doubt he needed to do much training in the Freudian stuff to master the art of effective head-shrinking. Many believe he "psyched" out the cricketing opposition anyway.

I asked him a question about this – not the psychoanalysis, but the cricket – over dinner at the Carlton Club after his talk. "Why at Headingley, in 1981, when we had so few runs to play with in the fourth innings, did you put on our best strike bowler, Bob Willis, toiling up the hill into the wind?"

"Funny you should ask that. Bob asked me the same question at the time. I told him, 'To make you angry.'"

Bob did get angry and England won.

Michael's talk was illuminating, witty and brilliantly expressed. He has a deep compassion for the suffering – especially the mental and spiritual suffering – of his fellow human beings. But, I confess, I wanted him to give up on Oedipus and catharsis and tell us what he thought of Lillee and Thomson.

Sometimes you write to ask someone to come and address the congregation with not much lively hope that they will accept. It was so when I wrote to invite the gifted actress Dame Diana Rigg to read T.S.Eliot's The Waste Land at our Ash Wednesday Choral Evensong. But she wrote back by return to say she would be delighted to come and do it; though, as a thorough professional, she insisted that she would first have to go up to Oxford and consult with the leading Eliot scholars concerning the poem's meaning. Such astonishing generosity to go to those lengths for a mere "church do". It wasn't as if she were going on stage at the Old Vic.

I was at church an hour before the service was due to start and from the top of the steps I could see across into the café on the other side of Cornhill where Diana was sitting, going over her lines. She came over to the vestry in good time and I told her of our tradition to have a few glasses of Malmsey wine after the Ash Wednesday service. Our Parish Clerk said, "Perhaps Dame Diana would like a glass now – for her throat's sake?"

"Oh, my dear boy, I'd simply love one!"

It turned out that Diana, like myself, came from Leeds and we began a programme of serial reminiscence and terminal nostalgia before the service started. After the wonderful singing of Allegri's Miserere and the matchless Funeral Sentences by Henry Purcell, Diana ascended the pulpit and began:

April is the cruellest month, breeding lilacs out of the dead land...

There followed twenty-five minutes of the most spellbinding recitation that I, or anyone else in the church, had ever heard. She read it as if she had written it, articulating with uncanny insight all the various moods of the greatest poem of the 20th century: the humorous, demotic stuff about Madame Sosostris and Hurry up please; it's time!...the unbearable wistfulness of Sweet Thames flow softly till I end my song...the apocalyptic section about fear in a handful of dust. It was more than a great theatrical experience: it was a spiritual experience.

I mentioned Diana's generosity. Well, it knew no bounds. It so happened that her daughter, also an actress, was making her West End debut that evening. Yet Diana had still agreed to come to St Michael's.

131

I tried to get a taxi for her straight after the service, so that she could get to the theatre where her daughter was appearing. Of course, at seven o'clock in the evening, all the taxis going west are taken. After several minutes' frustration, I had an inspiration: I flagged down a taxi, opened the door and asked the passengers, "Would either of you two gentlemen mind sharing a taxi with Diana Rigg?"

Well, what do you think?! So off she went.

Diana began a tradition for reading Eliot which we keep going at St Michael's. The following year, the celebrated tenor Robert Tear agreed to come and read Ash Wednesday. He read so beautifully – as if he were singing it. Not only did he read for us but, a few months later, he came one Sunday morning and preached an amazingly erudite and stimulating sermon at the Parish Eucharist. Here's a short extract from what he said that day:

"Ever since I can remember I have always wished to walk into an art gallery, a museum, even a spiritual building, and find no description of the pictures, objects or creeds. Alas! My desire has never been fulfilled and I find that in these places I am not only informed of what the objects are but also, often, what I should think of them. In fact, my (possibly) innocent eye, ear, soul has been influenced by the opinions of others. I find myself under the often malign influence of curators; how many times were we told that Mozart was pretty, Bach mechanical, van Gogh unstable? A custodian is of course a welcome creature, especially when she or he represents the law. When a citizen offends against the rules of society, such an officer rightly protects my liberty. A curator is, however, a different beast. The curator we most readily recognise is the keeper (or even custodian) of a collection of artefacts. In 1450 or so a curator (hence curate) was one who appointed as guardian of a minor or lunatic among others, but above all was one who had the cure of souls in his palm.

My plea for the non-defining of things springs from my belief that each object, each picture, each soul, each epiphany is unique in itself. The instant recognition (or repulsion) between the object and the observer I choose to define as the Spirit, or God, the Holy Ghost, or IT, the Paraclete or even the NO-THING. The possibility of this endless alliance of LOVE has never left my singular soul even in the darkest of vales."

It would be a blessing if more of the clergy could preach with such warmth and insight.

In Advent, I usually ask for distinguished visiting scholars to come and talk to us about the subjects which are our traditional meditation in that season leading directly up to Christmas. The topics are, of course, The Four Last Things: Death, Judgement, Hell and Heaven. One Advent, I invited Professor Roger Homan, from the School of Education in the University of Brighton. I have known Roger for years to be an outstanding scholar in the sociology of religion, a more than competent theologian and a devastating raconteur. Sure enough, he began his sermon – I can't at this distance in time remember whether it was on hell or heaven – with an anecdote.

Roger is almost totally blind. He began by telling us about his summer holiday in Greece and of how he went one day into a fine historic church there and had the vague sense that there were other visitors round about him. He muddled his way up the aisle, he said, and suddenly became conscious of a priest by his side – a priest who, he could just detect, was wearing a finely embroidered and very long cotta or surplice. The priest halted at the chancel step and Roger stopped beside him. It was a few minutes later, and only when a man had gently led him away, that he realised that he had been walking up the aisle with a bride.

A friend who returns again and again to speak to us at St Michael's is David Martin, a priest and one of the most eminent professors of sociology of religion in the world. Two of his sermons stand out in my memory. In one, he spoke about a painting in which the Christ Child with his mother is featured with a bunch of grapes and a sheaf of corn: those images being stark prophecies of the Body and the Blood of Calvary and hence of the Blessed Sacrament. And in the other sermon, David was making a similar point to that made by Robert Tear who so disliked having works of art explained to him.

David told the story of how Beethoven once played his great Appassionata piano sonata in public. When he had finished and the applause had died down, a young woman came up to him and said, "Herr Beethoven, that was certainly very fine – but what does it mean?"

Whereupon Beethoven said nothing, shrugged, sat down and played it again.

A Cup of Tea at the BBC

The BBC has been broadcasting religious programmes for eighty years and a producer invited me to Broadcasting House to tell them what I thought of the output. There is one aspect of programme policy that should not be allowed to go un-remarked. Whenever BBC television produces a programme about Christianity, the tone and content are all sceptical and debunking. You know the kind of thing: the allegation that we can't trust the biblical narratives, that Jesus was just an ordinary rabbi, that the resurrection did not happen but is only some sort of metaphor for the disciples' experience of "new life" and so on. But notice the contrast when the religion in question is, say, Islam or Buddhism: then the tone is reverential to the point of sycophancy as political correctness decrees that no stray word of criticism be allowed to intrude.

They stick the earphones on you and hand you a cup of instant coffee in a plastic cup. "What do you think of the BBC's television coverage of religion?"

I said I think that religion on television is generally unspeakable. There is the terminal nostalgia of Songs of Praise and Sunday morning's The Heaven and Earth Show which doesn't seem to be able to make up its mind whether it's a chat show or an amateur talent contest. So that leaves radio. The main religious programme of the week is the Sunday morning service which follows the eight o'clock news.

On Sunday morning, I continued, I take my wife a cup of tea up to bed and then come back downstairs to drink my own. We have a competition which begins at ten past eight to see who can switch the radio off quickest, before the morning service starts.

In my view, a religious service should be just that: an act of worship, not a mixture of chat show and travelogue. It should begin without announcement, but with a hymn. This should lead into a prayer, perhaps a psalm a reading, another hymn, the Creed and an intelligent sermon. Instead what we get is a long prologue of the, "I'm standing in the chancel of St Mungo's..." (Who cares?) "...There has been a church at St Mungo's since 1551, blah blah..."

I warmed to the theme. There's nothing religious about this

approach. It simply kills any potential spiritual atmosphere from the start. There's too much of the minister telling us what we are about to do next: 'We shall now say the words of the Creed..." Why not just begin, "I believe in God?" Or "We shall now confess our sins..." instead of "We have erred and strayed..." The result is that the irritating commentary becomes more important than the actual words of the service.

The form of the service is usually mindless: "Our music this morning is provided by the pupils of Bog Street Comprehensive who will accompany the singers on their Peruvian nose flutes."

And the hymns – I mean songs – dammit, I mean choruses after the style of:

I'm jumping for Jesus, jumping for Jesus, jumping for Jesus, Yes!

With the second verse of rather more exalted intellectual content:

I'm jogging for Jesus, jogging for Jesus, jogging for Jesus, Yes!

The readings are always from unspeakably awful modern translation, which reduce the biblical message to extreme banality. The sermon is invariably patronising and dumbed-down. It is well known that BBC producers and presenters are told as part of their training, "Assume no knowledge." But if you treat your listeners as idiots, they will either take justifiable offence and switch off or else they will participate in the idiocy and become idiots themselves. Why doesn't the BBC notice that the churches which are flourishing are the ones which use traditional language and liturgy: those Roman churches where they have the Latin Mass, and Anglican churches like our church of St Michael's, Cornhill, where we have The Book of Common Prayer. The Eastern Orthodox haven't altered their liturgy for a thousand years and their churches are packed.

I was asked to comment on the weekday output.

"Every weekday morning at ten to eight, we are offered Thought for the Day. This is always – except when the Chief Rabbi is occasionally allowed to present it – a brief essay in soft-left politics in which the speaker attempts to scold the government for its attitude towards the for example, war in Iraq/asylum seekers/women's rights/gay rights/the minimum wage – pick any three from four. I must say that the people who offer this advice every morning can hardly claim expertise. Bishops, synods-people most of them, have failed in every area of church life these last forty years. They have brought in new liturgies and the pews have emptied. They have lost so much money that they now confess openly they do not have enough cash to pay the clergy. Theological education is as dumbed down as an episode of Blue Peter. Seeing they are so manifestly incompetent when it comes to running their own affairs, it's a bit thick when they tell the politicians how to run theirs.

"Never mind, we can tolerate a bit of soft left soft soap and the slogans of ill-informed apparatchiks. What gets me is that they have been talking like this for forty years, yet they market this procession of clichés and hand-me-downs as if it were the cutting edge of social criticism. They have the ignorance and arrogance to describe this old hat as 'prophecy'. Eyes have they and see not, ears and hear not; and their feet are far from the paths of godliness.

"I hardly blame the BBC for this nonsense and bias. I'm convinced it's not done consciously. BBC types simply pick up the standard BBC mindset as they learn their trade – the whole repertoire of unexamined prejudices which they, however, regard as the hallmark of an open mind. Socrates said, 'The unexamined life is not worth living.' It's not worth broadcasting either."

I don't think they'll invite me back.

There Were Giants:
A Recollection of Fr John Paul R.I.P.

Father John Paul was an Australian, about five feet four inches tall in his high heels and one of the most gifted and powerful priests the City of London has ever seen. He came in 1986 from being Vicar of Balham in south London to be Rector of St James, Garlickhythe and St Andrew's by the Wardrobe. St James' is the headquarters of the Prayer Book Society and John was a stalwart.

In the early 1990s, the Church of England in the diocese of London found itself in the not unfamiliar situation of being short of money. The hierarchy got together and reasoned that the cause for this impoverishment was at least partly because there are forty-two ancient churches in the City – too many for the square mile which, in any case, has no resident population. So they decided to appoint a commission to - let us not put too fine a point on it – find an excuse for shutting down these expensive and underused resources. Lord Templeman was nominated as chairman and in due course a report was published which said that most of the churches should be closed down and sold off for livery halls. There is always a queue of livery companies looking for their own premises in the City.

The scheme envisaged four or five churches left operating, the number of clergy reduced drastically and the ecclesiastical organisation remodelled on something that looked like Berlin before the breaking down of the wall: four sectors with a senior clergyman in overall authority and a few assistant priests under him.

John Paul was disgusted by this reductionism, this abandonment, as he saw it, of the Church's mission in the most influential area of the nation's life. So he wrote to the Corporation of London and all the livery companies to let them know what was afoot. He gathered a small but highly intelligent and informed group of people and produced his own report to answer the Templeman Enquiry's findings. This report was called, quoting St Paul's letter to the Corinthians, A More Excellent Way. The Guildhall was booked and all the movers and shakers in the City assembled to discuss the crisis.

The consensus was that as many as possible of the churches should be kept open, and that money should be found to guarantee this by various ways and means. Happily, at about the same time, a new Bishop was appointed to London, The Rt Rev'd and Rt Honourable Richard Chartres, who shared the vision of open churches throughout the City professing a ministry to the financial sector. It was a great victory for John Paul and a triumph for his visionary approach.

I arrived in London in 1998. My immediate past experience was of two country parishes in Yorkshire, and what I knew about the workings of the City of London could have been written on the back of a credit transfer note. My wife and I were sitting in the Watch House one evening when there was a knock at the door and I answered it to find John Paul standing there. He entered with a bottle of wine and said, "Welcome to the City. I'd like to tell you one or two things you'll need to know."

Never have I been so grateful for an hour's conversation. He explained the structure of the City's government: the Lord Mayor, the Aldermen, the Common Councilmen, the place of the liveries; and he told me how to avoid putting my foot in it.

Not long after this, John invited me to speak to his advanced Sunday School – a delightful title for what was really an afternoon lecture society held in his church. First my wife and I were treated to lunch, fabulously prepared and presented by John's wife, Lynette. I remember it was delicious and I ate so much that I was in danger of falling asleep during my own lecture! I spoke on the need to keep The Book of Common Prayer in regular use at the main services of the Church, and I also argued for Establishment – the historic link between Church and state – to be preserved. "Otherwise," I said, "the Church will decline from being an institution for everyone in England into a mere sect for enthusiasts." I added, "There is, believe it or not, a bishop in our Church – not the Bishop of London – who is very keen to disestablish the Church. I suppose I'd better not name him."

Putting my lily-liveredness to shame, John broke in at once and said, "I'll name him: Colin Buchanan!" John's fingering of this Episcopal disestablishmentarian was all the more telling for the vigorous Aussie tone in which it was uttered: "I'll nime 'im!"

In 2000, John retired from the full-time ministry, but sadly and very soon afterwards he was diagnosed with cancer of the oesophagus – a painful, distressing and lingering illness which he bore with typical fortitude and cheerfulness. And during this last period of his life, he still kept up in the press his customary polemical criticisms of a Church hierarchy which he generally saw as having surrendered to the secular liberalism of the age.

The Corporation Church of St Lawrence, Jewry was packed for John's funeral. The service was traditional: The Burial of the Dead from The Book of Common Prayer. The singing was lusty and patriotic: I Vow to Thee My Country. It began with Rupert Brooke's poem, evocative of England, The Soldier, and continued with music by Edward Elgar.

John's son and daughter paid short, delightful, un-sycophantic tributes to their father and the Bishop of London gave the main address. In it he recalled that John in his final illness had asked a visitor, "Why am I having to linger on so long?"

His friend, the visitor, paused for a moment, then said, "Well, you see, John...all those open letters you sent to bishops and synods, all your letters to the papers – I suppose St Peter can't stand to think of all the controversy!"

The Order of Service had the Cross of St George emblazoned on the front. The triumphal music at the end included William Walton's Spitfire Prelude. The last words on the Order were: "He loved England as he loved the Church of England." I thought of John, his courage and his kindness; and a phrase leapt into my head, "Who are these like stars appearing?"

Choirs and Places Where They Sing

Sir Thomas Beecham said, "The English people don't know much about music, but they sure like the sound it makes." This is also true of the English and church music. Roger Scruton offers a very evocative description of the effect of traditional organ music in church:

"During the administration of Holy Communion, the organist would improvise on muted pipes, whimsical watery sequences, full of fifths and fourths in the manner of Vaughan Williams and Herbert Howells. It was as if the Holy Ghost himself were present, humming quietly to himself in an English accent."

The only quarrel I have with Roger about those words is his use of "as if." It is a matter of principle among congregations to object fiercely if they are presented with a hymn they don't already know. There is no remedy for this. It is what happens with all congregations everywhere. The only thing the rector can say is, "Well, just remember, there was a time when you didn't know Onward Christian Soldiers" and hope for the best.

The English are fortunate in that there is a treasury of easy-to-sing hymns which fits perfectly with the traditional services in The Book of Common Prayer and which draws heavily, almost exclusively, on the sublime language of The King James Bible. Nearly all the traditional and best-loved hymns are full of quotes from, or evocations of, the old Bible: "Abide with me" – from the walk to Emmaus; "the steep and rugged pathway" - from the parables of Jesus; "O Sacred Head" – from the terrible story of the crucifixion. So, the hymns are the historic and habitual way in which Christians have been taught the faith: they teach themselves as they sing week by week.

There is a pervasive myth to the effect that relationships between the Rector and the organist are usually fraught. This is enshrined in many jokes, such as, "What's the difference between an organist and a terrorist?"

"You can negotiate with a terrorist."

It's cruel and it's an exaggeration – but, as with all exaggerations, there's a bit of truth in it. My first Vicar really hated music in church and regarded it as a distraction. I remember being asked to help with the choir practices while the proper organist was on holiday one August. I made the mistake of introducing, into the singing of familiar hymns, tunes they had not sung before. I did this because I believed that some tunes would be an improvement on what we had been used to: for example, the Bach tune to Bread of Heaven. When the Vicar came back and heard in the Sunday service what we had been practising, I was on the edge of getting the sack.

When I was a country parson with two Yorkshire villages to look after, I was fortunate to have as my organist Thomas "Tim" Tunnard, who, as a boy at Windsor, had trained under Walford Davies. Tim was former Master of the Music at Birmingham Cathedral. Evensong was unforgettable: I would stand facing the congregation to give the Blessing at the end of the service, the sunset pouring through the coloured lights of the west window and Tim playing The Day Thou Gavest Lord is Ended/The Darkness Falls at Thy Behest and altering the harmonies and inflection of each verse to represent musically the differing sentiments being expressed. It was a miracle of evocation. You felt you were being immersed in English religious sensibility. After funerals, he would always play the matchless C-minor last chorus from Bach's St Matthew Passion. As he said, "It's the only thing you could play." And after the service we would withdraw to The Chequers or The White Swan and drink away "the bier money". We made a custom of doing the same on Ash Wednesday as well: in the Commination we would, as Tim put it, "...curse all and sundry and then go off to the pub." It certainly got Lent off to a good start!

In my City churches we have a fine musical tradition and a big set piece Choral Eucharist and not least of the reasons why our churches are so well-sought after for weddings and memorial services is the quality of the music. We also continue Harold Darke's long-running series of Monday organ recitals.

There are choirs and there are choirs. Luckily, we have one that is house-trained, but I have known City churches where the singers don't act as if they are the choir of the parish church, but as some privileged visiting choral society come to exhibit their exquisite artistry and to be otherwise waited on hand and foot. I feel sorry for those Rectors who have to endure this sort of prima-donna-ism and all the disturbance that it causes, with an accompanying lack of etiquette. Some choristers are unable to endure for more than five minutes without a swig from a bottle of mineral water or a munch on a biscuit. And I have been taken into colleagues' churches where the choir vestries are a shambles of half-empty water bottles and partly-eaten packets of biscuits – left, presumably, pour encourager les souris. I was even introduced to one Director of Music and told that he thought nothing of phoning the Rector's wife at half past nine on a Sunday morning to say, "We're here rehearsing, and there's no toilet paper in the loo. Bring some with you when you come to the service!" In some such unfortunate places there is a colossal arrogance.

Individual musicians are famously idiosyncratic. After more than thirty years as a parish priest, I could write a complete Who's Who? of musical characters. There was, for example, a weird American organist who asked if he might give a recital at St Sepulchre's while he was on a tour of the British Isles. Well, yes, we try to be accommodating. It emerged that he wanted not only the opportunity to play our celebrated organ for the customary applause and modest expenses, but to be paid a professional fee, to have someone to turn the music for him, to be provided with several meals at the Rectory while he lodged with me for two nights. Well, what can you say?

He did not even play the organ particularly appealingly. There are, I have discovered, two sorts of organists: in the minority are the genuinely musical; then you have the nerds, the anoraks, those who have the same sort of pathological obsession with the instrument that others have with steam trains. This sort plays the organ not as if it was a musical instrument, but a primitive type of traction-engine.

They say that parsons are like manure: spread thinly over a large area, they do a lot of good; but if you get a lot of them all together in one place, they stink to high heaven. The same can certainly be said of organists. We once held the annual meeting of the Royal College of Organists at St Michael's. What this sort likes best is sentimental 19th century organ and choral music by obscure performers: full of diminished chords, what I call, "Come into the garden, Lord, music." There are critical, spiritual descriptions of this disease: it seems to me morbid, self-seeking, derivative, cynical and atheistic – the ideal religious music, one might say, for those who have no religion. The church is full of musical devotees of this stuff: musicians who imagine that church music can exist without the faith for which it was composed as accompaniment; who think that they possess a higher sensibility than the faith once delivered to the saints.

There was the long-winded piling-up of fake art masquerading as piety. One requires no emetic. I wonder, to take just one example, how anyone calling himself a musician could think for a moment of "adorning" the sublime Thomas Tallis with Barnby: "Sweet and awful," one might say. And who put the "limp" in Limpus? It was like being at a memorial service for an old aunt you'd never met. A single honest blast of Tallis, Byrd, Haydn or Mozart would have blown away instantly all those miserable cobwebs. Or it was like a fastidious and long-drawn-out Masonic.

Speaking of that "colossal arrogance," I was peremptorily greeted at that RCO meeting by Richard Popplewell, the predecessor and former teacher of our Director of Music at St Michael's. Without a trace of humour, hyperbole or irony, he said, "Your Director of Music is very pleased with you."

"Oh really? Thank you. I'm so glad to hear it!"

Anyhow, the American anorak stayed and ate us out of house and home. He also turned out to have a very short fuse and an alarming susceptibility to strong drink. He went out late one afternoon and came back mid-evening. I offered him a drink and he drank three or four. Then he got riled. I should mention that the evening before I had visiting The Watch House the distinguished organist and superlative composer and all-round musician Francis Jackson who had not long before retired from his post of Master of the Music at York Minster. The weird American organist had been in for supper the same evening and he was excessively, even creepily, sycophantic towards Francis, constantly expressing exaggerated and embarrassing admiration for his talent.

But by the following evening, Francis had gone home. When the weird organist had drunk a few drinks, he began his discourse on English church music, which he said was "Crap. And the crappiest of the lot is Francis Jackson."

143

"That's not what you said last night." At first he ignored my remark. Then:

"I don't care what I said last night. It's all crap I tell you."

I suppose I should have said simply, "Well, thank you, and good-night", but his abusiveness – not to say his hypocrisy – drove me on to make replies that were no doubt injudicious:

"What, Elgar, Walford Davies, Herbert Howells, Vaughan Williams, Benjamin Britten, William Walton – all crap, are they?"

"Yeah. Of course they're crap!"

"How about the European masters: Mozart, Haydn, Mendelssohn..." I got no further –

"All f****** crap!"

I was too far in now to withdraw. I said, "I see. Then is there anyone who isn't f****** crap?"

His face took on the rosy look of inebriated ecstasy: "Hindemith!" I'm afraid I couldn't resist misquoting Thomas Beecham, "Oh, I've not heard a great deal of Hindemith – but I think I once trod in some."

That was it. He yelled, "I'm not taking any more of this! I'm going to bed! I'll be down for my breakfast at eight." And he stumbled nois-ily up the stairs. There was a great deal of banging and clattering before, at length, everything was fell quiet.

When I got up next morning, the bathroom was suffused with the intense fragrance of my wife's perfume – excessively so, as if some-one had emptied out the whole bottle. Actually, this judgement was not far wrong: the bottle was missing, and with it one of our hand towels. Well, I went downstairs and set out the things for breakfast. At about half past eight, the weird organist appeared, red in the face, at the top of the stairs from where he threw down his travelling trunk with a great crash.

"Come on down and have some breakfast!"

A terrific shout from the staircase: "I will eat nothing in this house!"

Well, that, at least, was a reverse of his previous policy. My wife showed him to the bus stop and we giggled all morning, happy in the knowledge that we had seen (and heard) the last of him. But there was a sequel. A week or so later, I was due to give an after-dinner speech to one of the City Ward Clubs at the Baltic Exchange. When the for-mal proceedings were over, one of the members of the Ward Club came across and said, "Are you going to have a visit from an American organist who's touring the country?"

"We had him the other week?"

"What was it like?"

"Interesting."

"We had him last night."

"What was it like?

"Interesting. When he'd gone, were you missing anything?"

"A bottle of perfume and a towel. How about you?"

"Only a bottle of gin."

I mentioned Francis Jackson. A consummate musician and a sheer delight to have around. He's eighty-five now and quite unstoppable. I asked him to come and give a recital for us and stay a few days. It was quite a trek for him. He has retired to Malton in Yorkshire, so he had to get up at five in the morning, catch the bus to York, the train to King's Cross, the tube to Farringdon, then walk the half mile to the Watch House. He still managed to sit in an armchair and smile like a mischievous cherub. He drank coffee and nattered to me for an hour. The he went to practise the organ for his recital, found the organ broken, mended it, gave a brilliant recital, ate a good lunch with no niggardly amount of white wine before announcing that he was off on the bus to spend the afternoon in the National Gallery.

That evening, I had to go to a Church Council meeting and when I returned Francis was just finishing supper. He was obviously in the mood for some music. I asked him if he knew the Mozart Coronation Mass and he replied in his gentle, innocent tone, "Oh no – I've never heard of it."

I was taken in completely, and I reached into the piano stool and pulled out the score. He looked at it briefly, then closed it up before beginning to play the Mozart with verve and sparkle – including all the descending fast quavers in the left hand in octaves.

In addition to the trials, there is so much fun in church music and many charming surprises. Two of the best of these featured visiting schools' choirs: one from Italy who sang an operatic selection – including an ambitious and scintillating performance by a fourteen-year-old of The Queen of the Night's second aria from Die Zauberflote; and another, highly musical and impeccably well-mannered visit by The

Houston, Texas, Children's Choir, performing Schubert, Bach, Gounod and American spirituals.
Angel voices ever singing...angel harps forever ringing...

"To Do a Good Action by Stealth and Have it Found Out by Accident"

According to Charles Lamb, that is the greatest blessing anyone can receive. I reckon he was a saint, having looked after his insane, murderous sister all his life. At the time when he promised the magistrate that he would act as her guardian and surety all his days, he was engaged to be married. He gave up his fiancée and from that day renounced any hope of love.

So I'm proud of Lamb's bust on the front of The Watch House, even though this means that during evenings and weekends we are paid many visits by City Guides and their tourist customers. The guides relate Lamb's story in a loud voice – and almost invariably they get the details wrong.

Lamb was a wit of the surreal sort, and I often think he would fit admirably into the cast of Monty Python. He had a broad taste in black humour and once said, "Anything awful makes me laugh. I misbehaved once at a funeral."

He was extremely sociable, clubbable and seemed always to be at dinner somewhere with literary and artistic friends. At one of these dinners, Coleridge was holding forth as usual. He paused, turned to Lamb for support, and said, "I believe you've heard me preach, Charles?"

"Why," said Lamb, "I never heard you do anything else!"

Wordsworth was forever trying to get him to walk in the Lakeland fells, but Charles would have none of it. He said, "You can keep your mountains. I love to live in other men's minds. I love reading. I cannot sit and think. Books think for me."

When he did go for a walk, he paced himself in an extraordinary and idiosyncratic style. He never walked by the mile, but always by how much drink he thought he deserved for the distance covered. So he would say to Thomas Hood, with whom he rambled often: "Now I have walked a pint."

147

Hood said, "Walking with him was like going on a walk with Izaak Walton – minus the fishing."

The Charles Lamb Society sometimes comes to St Sepulchre's for its literary gatherings, when members give short talks about the great man. Twenty or thirty men and women, all of a certain age: it is these little societies that do more than anything else – and certainly more than the academic study of literature - to keep the love of English letters alive. They came the other year and, after the short talks, we processed outside to the east end of the church and I blessed Lamb's memorial. I felt he would have approved. The statue of Charles Lamb came to St Sepulchre's from Christ Church Greyfriars which was the church attended by Christ's Hospital School. Christ's Church was almost totally destroyed by Hitler's bombs and the shell of it is in our parish, so I suppose it was only right that the memorial should come to us.

Long ago, the school moved out of the City to Horsham in Sussex, but they returned to St Sepulchre's last year for their Annual Service to mark the 450th anniversary of their founding. It was a delight to have all those talented boys and girls in church, and their singing and instrumental playing was a fair way above the standard usually expected of schoolchildren. The only disappointment, at least as far as I was concerned, was that the music master chose to have them play and sing the Te Deum by John Rutter. As everyone knows, the Te Deum ends with the heartfelt prayer, "Let me never be confounded." Surely only John Rutter could so score his musical setting that the word "confounded" occurs on a fortissimo! What, for heaven's sake, is this supposed to indicate – triumphant despair or the good news of our damnation?

I mentioned the little literary societies as the living stream which keeps English letters alive by their regular readings and informal talks. One of the members of the Charles Lamb Society, Leslie Irons, went even better and wrote a two-act drama on the essayist's life entitled Lamb's Tale: My Gentle-Hearted Charles. It played to a large audience one summer Saturday's afternoon in St Sepulchre's.

That's the sort of thing for which you think the City churches were intended. It brought Lamb home, where he belongs. His words shone out through Leslie's clever script. As the late afternoon sun filtered dustily through the west window, you could think you glimpsed gentle-hearted Charles in the shadows, applauding discreetly.

Also by Peter Mullen

(FICTION - NOVELS)
Blessed Assurance
Only A Lad
Growing Up With Sex and Death

(FICTION – SHORT STORIES)
Rural Rites
Country Matters
Holy and Unholy Ghosts
Haunted Lives

(NON-FICTION)
Beginning Philosophy
Thinking About Religion
Working With Morality
Being Saved: A Comparison of Christian Theology and Jungian
Psychology
The New Babel
Dreams That Come True
Reason To Believe
Death Be Not Proud
A History of the Promenade Concerts
Shrines of Our Lady
Verse & Worse

(EDITED)
No Alternative: A Guide to the Prayer Book Controversy
Strange Gifts: The Charismatic Movement in the Church of England
Unholy Warfare: The Church & The Bomb
Faking It: The Sentimentalisation of Society
The Real Common Worship